ENERGIZING your CHILDREN'S MINISTRY

CYNTHIA BROWN

Published by Concordia Publishing House
3558 S. Jefferson Ave., St. Louis, MO 63118-3968
1-800-325-3040 • www.cph.org

Library of Congress Cataloging-in-Publication Data

Names: Brown, Cynthia Stokes, author.
Title: Energizing your children's ministry / Cynthia Brown.
Description: St. Louis : Concordia Pub. House, 2016. | Includes
    bibliographical references and index.
Identifiers: LCCN 2016008217 (print) | LCCN 2016009724 (ebook) | ISBN
    9780758654953 (alk. paper) | ISBN 9780758654960 ()
Subjects: LCSH: Church work with children. | Christian education of children.
Classification: LCC BV639.C4 B76 2016 (print) | LCC BV639.C4 (ebook) | DDC
    259/.22--dc23
LC record available at http://lccn.loc.gov/2016008217

1 2 3 4 5 6 7 8 9 10   25 24 23 22 21 20 19 18 17 16

PRAISE FOR
ENERGIZING YOUR CHILDREN'S MINISTRY
··

Energizing Your Children's Ministry is an excellent resource for churches seeking to understand how to organize their children's ministry. Leaders who are either new to ministry, revitalizing their children's ministry, or desiring to train their teams to better understand the scope of children's ministry will benefit from this quality resource.

—Dr. David L. Rueter, Associate Professor of Christian Education
and DCE Program Director, Concordia University Irvine
Author of *Teaching the Faith at Home* (CPH 2016)

Cynthia Brown invites you to grab a cup of coffee and sit down for an intriguing discussion in an often overlooked area of the church—children's ministry. You may wonder what questions you would ask this veteran of frontline ministry with children and their families. But no worries—she supplies fourteen critical questions (and answers) which guide the children's ministry novice, volunteer, veteran, or professional on a journey that will energize ministry with children and their families. Professor Brown outlines a biblically based, relationally focused process, which helps you develop direction, plan and organize, recruit and train others, to move your vision forward in children's ministry!

—Dr. Steve Christopher, Family Life Program Director
Concordia University Ann Arbor

Wouldn't it be incredible if every child and family the Lord gave us the opportunity to serve was welcomed warmly, taught with joyful enthusiasm, and excited to participate every Sunday and bring their friends? If your children's ministry needs some energizing, this book by Cynthia Brown could become your new best friend with resources and blueprints for considering and guiding change. Every family ministry or children's ministry leader (lay or professional) would benefit from reading it personally and then recruiting a group of committed volunteers to read it together and begin looking at positive steps that can be taken to energize children's ministry in the local congregation. One size doesn't fit all, and the people best equipped to solve the challenges of ministry are those who live it every week in their own church. This book can help with that.

This is a timeless and timely book designed to help all of us "up our game" so that precious children are brought to Jesus without hindrance. I can't wait to order multiple copies and get a group going to consider how we might better serve families and energize ministry to children at my church. Thank you to Cynthia Brown and Concordia Publishing House for a book that brings research, ideas, and practical wisdom all together in one place for all of us to use!

—Jill Hasstedt, DCE
Zion Lutheran Church and School
Belleville, Illinois

Table of Contents

Dedicated to my grandsons, Elliott and Ian.
May the love you now have for Jesus remain
with you throughout your lives.

Preface

"Equip the saints for the work of ministry, for building up the
body of Christ." Ephesians 4:12

Hello there! Let's grab a cup of coffee and talk children's ministry. You may be a brand-new leader or a longtime volunteer "promoted" to leader status, or maybe God ignited a fire within you to more effectively reach kids and their families for Christ. Whatever the role God has given you, I am thankful for your willingness to say yes! Whether it is a bold yes or a hesitant one doesn't matter—God equips those He calls. I would love to walk the journey of discovery in children's ministry with you. People from many churches have contacted me through the years, asking for guidance. So let's imagine that we are sitting down together, talking and listening to one another, seeking ways to creatively reach kids and their families with the good news of the Gospel.

I admit to being biased. My bias is that children's ministry is one of the most important ministries a church can offer, if not the most important. As Elizabeth Browning penned, "Let me count the ways." First of all, we know God thinks children are important because He instructs parents to teach them about Him from morning to night among the tasks of each day (Deuteronomy 6:4–9; Psalm 78:1–8). We also recall the value Jesus places on children with

His welcome and blessing in the face of the disciples' rebuke (Mark 10:13–16). Jesus goes so far as to say that He reveals mysteries to children that are hidden from the wise (Matthew 11:25). He challenges adults to change and to humbly reflect childlike hearts (Matthew 18:2–6). Anyone who welcomes a child actually welcomes Jesus (v. 5)! Warnings follow about punishment for anyone who causes a child to sin (v. 6).

Have you noticed that relationships with Jesus begin more often in children than in adults? (It would be wonderful, however, if we also witnessed more adult Baptisms in church). Barna Research supports this observation as well. "By age nine, most children have their spiritual moorings in place," writes George Barna in *Transforming Children into Spiritual Champions*.[1] So let's start young! The foundational values that are laid will have a lifetime impact.

If you're not already convinced of the importance of children's ministry, consider this: parents can be reached through their children. Many parents sat through an evening VBS program or proudly watched their children sing in church only to have their own disconnected hearts surprisingly touched by the Spirit. Yes, God's kingdom can grow through what churches offer children.

Raising kids in our world is not getting any easier, and supporting families can be a blessing to moms, dads, and caregivers. Parents look for healthy, safe, enriching activities that they and their children can enjoy. The local YMCA or Boys and Girls Club offer many options, but churches can create opportunities that make an eternal impact! Invitational outreach programs can help transition moms and dads to become part of the church body that understands God's desires for them in their role as parents. We have the opportunity to partner with those who have not been discipled by their own parents and who may not know how to spiritually guide their children.

Yes, children can be the route to a parent's heart. In a world where relationships are fragmented, families are hurting, and violence fills the news, a place where a message of hope, peace, and love is taught can offer a sacred space of respite for families.

Finally, children's ministry provides opportunities for connection. Neuroscientists and psychologists alike observe and write about humanity's intrinsic need for relationship. Caring parents want their children to develop healthy

---

1   George Barna, *Transforming Children into Spiritual Champions* (Ventura, CA: Regal Books, 2003), 14.

friendships; church leaders can respond by intentionally promoting Christian fellowship in their classes. Having friends at their place of worship helps kids (and their parents) remain connected with the church as well as its people.

This sense of connection also extends to those who serve in children's ministry. Serving helps volunteers grow closer with one another and make an important contribution to their church family. For nearly two years, I made phone calls to people in our congregation who missed worship services for six weeks or more. I began the project anticipating that I would primarily be contacting young people in their twenties. To my amazement, the bulk of the calls were to people in their fifties and sixties. I learned that once their children grow up, people in this age group often become disconnected from church and lose their avenues of service. Because of the high need for volunteers to serve with children, opportunities for connection abound. Yes, indeed, the need for an active children's ministry is as great as ever!

So what exactly is children's ministry? The phrase is fairly recent, only emerging in past decades. Is it the same as Sunday School? VBS? preschool? Yes, yes, yes, and more! Children's ministry has many different faces—just as churches do. Children's ministry is a church's efforts to help children grow spiritually. It's an "umbrella phrase" that incorporates everything a church does for kids. In one church, it may simply mean Sunday School; in another, it may include children's choirs, sports programs, and family events. In another, it may represent kids' messages and child-friendly bulletins in "big church"; in still another, children's ministry may be defined by a Day School or Baptism classes. Great variety exists!

Many resources on the subject exist as well. There is no shortage of books equipping leaders in the areas of children's and family ministry. So why another book on the same topic now? The books that currently exist come from theological perspectives and publishing companies other than our own Lutheran Church—Missouri Synod. My Concordia University students and I need to use these sources because of their availability, but that includes correcting the theological differences such as Law and Gospel and the Sacraments to fit our Lutheran worldview. People working with children and families in our churches who are looking for practical guidance only have these non-Lutheran resources from which to choose. I hope to help fill that void.

In addition, hands-on opportunities for equipping and encouraging those volunteering with children and families have diminished within our church body. Dr. Dale Griffin and Dr. Judith Christian contributed decades of support and administration for VBS, Sunday School, preschools, children's ministry, and family ministry. Currently our church body does not have a department for Children's and Family Ministry. The last national synodical conference on children's ministry was held in 2011. Some districts still offer workshops, but they are infrequent. Even in my own Michigan District, our Children's Ministry Task Force was disbanded in 2007, leaving few remaining resources to support congregations in their work with children.

I care about children's leaders struggling in the trenches, unsure of where to seek guidance. I will never claim to have all the answers, but I have slugged in those trenches as well and continue to do so. My formal career with children began in 1971 as an elementary teacher at Peace Lutheran Church in Disco, Michigan (currently Shelby Township), along with other roles involving children. God eventually led our family to Faith Lutheran Church in Troy, Michigan, where I spent many years leading the Sunday School and eventually became the Children's Ministry Director. After an early retirement, I developed and continue to teach the core curriculum for the Children's Ministry Concentration in the Family Life Department at Concordia University Ann Arbor. Last year, my husband and I transferred our membership to St. Augustine Lutheran Church, also located in Troy, where I serve in a number of educational and leadership roles as a volunteer DCE. Hopefully, my experiences preparing Family Life Directors for the LCMS along with leading programs and serving people in both large and small churches will help me prepare you to more confidently and intentionally reach children and their families with the good news of the Gospel.

* * * *

I had walked away from church because of some bad experiences. Later, I felt the void in my life, and the Spirit led me back to church. I attended Faith because it was so big and I could go unnoticed. Worship and leave, just God and me. However, I know now that is not what God wanted. God planned for me to go to this church and put the right people in my life to help grow my faith and see the importance of community. My son at the time was four when he was amazed by Mr. Dan and his songs. Mr. Dan gave my son a high five after service and listened to this little boy tell him how he loved his music. The next week, Mr. Dan gave Omar a CD of that song. That moment touched my heart. Soon after, I signed my son up for the children's choir. I asked if I could stay and watch my son. The amazing volunteers welcomed me and enlisted my help. Through the course of the year working with the choir, the Holy Spirit moved in me, showing me the importance of gathering as a community of believers. I realized my former thought that it's just God and me is not what He intended. I soon was introduced to the children's ministry leader, Cynthia. I began volunteering, sharing my gifts with the children as she shared her gifts mentoring me.

C. J. Wajeeh
Faith Lutheran Church
Troy, MI

* * * *

Why Is Children's Ministry So Important?

1. God instructs parents to teach their children about Him (Deuteronomy 6:4–9 and Psalm 78:1–8).

2. Jesus welcomes and blesses children in the face of the disciples' rebuke (Mark 10:13–16).

3. Jesus reveals mysteries to children that are hidden from the wise (Matthew 11:25).

4. Jesus challenges adults to change and to humbly reflect childlike hearts (Matthew 18:2–6).

5. Jesus presents Himself to those who welcome children. Those who cause children to sin are punished (Matthew 18:5–6).

6. Most people enter a relationship with Jesus as children (George Barna).

7. Parents can be spiritually reached through their children.

8. Parents seek healthy, safe, enriching activities that they and their children can enjoy. Churches can create opportunities for this as well as add the spiritual component.

9. Churches can mentor parents who may not know how to spiritually guide their children.

10. Churches can offer a sacred space of respite for weary and hurting families.

11. Children's ministry provides opportunities for parents and children to develop friendships and connect with their peers.

12. Children's ministry allows volunteers to bond with one another and make a difference in the lives of other people.

Children's Ministry
at My Church

List all the ways your church supports children and their families through programs, activities, events, and services.

1. _____

2. _____

3. _____

4. _____

5. _____

6. _____

7. _____

8. _____

9. _____

10. _____

Where Do I Begin?

"Trust in the LORD with all your heart, and do not lean on your own understanding. In all your ways acknowledge Him, and He will make straight your paths." Proverbs 3:5–6

Are you ready to jump right in? Stop! Get on your knees first. God's kingdom is unlike man's and cannot be advanced on our own. My prayer is that we will work in step with Him, not march ahead nor lag behind. The only way I know how to keep in sync is to keep speaking with Him (praying) and listening to Him (remaining in the Word). Ministry cannot be about what *we* want, or even what *others* want; it is about what *God* wants. And an amazing thing happens when we surrender our agenda to Him—what *He* wants becomes what *we* want! That's how Jesus lived, and that's the life into which He invites us. When we rest in Him, priorities become clear, lesser things are more easily tossed aside, and sleep comes effortlessly at night.

Those of us go-getters (and I'm one of them) want to hit the ground running, generate change, and produce results. Results, however, are part of God's domain and may appear in ways least expected. So let's take a step back, pace ourselves, and start with our ABCDs—that is, we need to Assess, Build, Create, and Define. I'll describe these now and further develop the concepts in the pages to come.

ASSESS THE NEEDS

Several years ago, I attended a "School of Spiritual Direction" taught by Dr. Larry Crabb. One of his favorite questions was "Where is your red dot?" Using the image of the "you are here" location maps found at every mall, he invited us to consider what was going on in our lives at the present moment. That question applies to our formal ministry as well. We need to start with where we are before we try to make changes or transition to new ways of being or doing.

In order to assess your church's particular needs, start by being curious. Imagine that you are walking into your church for the very first time; take note of the sights, sounds, smells, and experiences. (See the checklist at the end of this chapter.) Observe, learn, listen, and evaluate. Each church building and each church community has its own culture or personality, its own way of doing things.

I have been a member of two different congregations within the same city recently, and the cultural differences are poignant. Different sizes, different median ages, different histories, different worship styles, different challenges, and different approaches to the inclusion of children in worship, only to mention a few. Our call is to discern what God wants to accomplish in and through His people in each unique setting. What works at one location may flop at another. It takes time to pray and to plan, focusing on God's gifts to your congregation and location. After all, He is the one who is leading!

Last fall when we were new members at our church, I noted a comment that the annual Harvest Bonfire was "only for our members." That surprised me; our pastor regularly encourages the congregation to invite friends and neighbors, and a bonfire seemed to be a perfect venue. Now, as we anticipate the event again, we've discussed adding activities for children and encouraging members to invite guests. Only God knows what the outcome will be, but one year later, attitudes toward "outsiders" will hopefully be different for this event.

Look around at your community as well. God placed your church here. These are the people that He called you to reach. Who are they? What are their needs? Has your church addressed the changes that have taken place through the years? Does your church population reflect the makeup of the residents in the neighborhoods surrounding your church?

The latest count in our city of Troy is eighty-three languages being spoken in our homes. Over one fourth of our community was born outside of this country. The majority of the children in our church's preschool are Korean. The names of many stores and restaurants near our home are written in Arabic. Do you see a theme? Pastors at both of our churches point out the need to pay attention to the changes around us and to embrace the mission field that has already come to us. Only ten miles south of us, huge, beautiful, empty Lutheran churches in the city of Detroit serve as sad reminders to earnestly seek how to address spiritual, physical, emotional, and economic needs right at our back doors.

And remember, just because you see a need doesn't mean you need to address it right away. Slow down your desire to "fix things," and trust in God to respond in His time and to work through you according to His will.

BUILD RELATIONSHIPS

We are people called to serve people, receive from people, and invite people to follow Jesus (Matthew 4:19). See the common denominator? People! We can't exist without them. Our pastor loves to refer to John Maxwell's "Law of Connection," which states, "Leaders touch a heart before they ask for a hand." In his *21 Laws of Irrefutable Leadership*, Maxwell says we connect with people when we make it a point to know their names, their personal stories, and their hopes and dreams.[2] As leaders, we must take the initiative with people. Our ministries are only as successful as our ability to relate to others. But note this warning for introverts like myself: be sure to protect your "alone time" so you have the energy required to move toward people. When I start thinking, "I'd love my job if it weren't for people," I know it's time to step away and be alone to pray with God for a while.

Connecting with people didn't originate with John Maxwell, of course. Jesus' ministry was all about relationships. First and foremost was His relationship with His Father, followed by His relationship with others. "You shall love the Lord your God with all your heart and with all your soul and with all your mind. This is the great and first commandment. And a second is like it:

---

2   John Maxwell, *21 Laws of Irrefutable Leadership* (Nashville: Thomas Nelson, 1998), p. 113.

17

You shall love your neighbor as yourself" (Matthew 22:37–39). Love for God is the most important relationship because it's our response to His initiating and overwhelming love for us. The love God has for us is the place from which we draw strength to love and serve Him and others. So who are the people God placed in our lives with whom we can grow?

» **Parents.** They are your partners and peers; getting to know them will help you know their needs and better understand their children. My college students sometimes express their trepidation at serving as Family Life Directors when they are young, single, and without children of their own. No one holds all wisdom, no matter how long they have been serving or how many children they have reared. In fact, parents often say that they knew more about parenting *before* they had children of their own. An attitude of humility regardless of our age or experience allows us to learn from others.

» **Children.** We need to know the youngsters we serve. Be approachable and get down to their eye level. Smile and ask open-ended questions. Bonding with children opens their hearts to receive our love, guidance, and correction. I always admired my sons' elementary school principal. She called each child by name when she greeted them in the halls or on the playground. As a parent in the school, I loved seeing her personally connect with those kids of mine who meant the world to me.

» **Volunteers.** Your ministry would simply not exist without the volunteers. Ministry is not a one-man or one-woman show; rather, it is a partnership. The myriad of volunteers are the ground troops who bring God-given plans to fruition. A word of caution: volunteers are serving God, not you or me. We should appreciate people for who they are, not what they do for us. A sense of being used will send volunteers right out the door, and it should!

» **Congregation.** They are fellow members of the Body of Christ. You most likely will represent children in their minds—what a high honor that is! Your role is to help them see kids and their families through the eyes of Jesus. And as you meet people, you may eventually help them find their own unique places of service that complement their strengths and gifts. You may discover prayer warriors, seamstresses, or former teachers. People want to know they are making a difference in the lives of others, and surely their gifts can fulfill ministry needs.

» **Pastor, church leadership, and boards.** These are the people to whom you will present your vision and your ideas with the hope that they will endorse and support your efforts. Be prepared to express how the purpose of children's ministry reinforces the purpose of the church at large. Communicate, communicate, communicate! As you keep people informed about your areas of responsibility, offer to support the efforts of your colleagues in their own roles as well.

» **Community.** Jesus and His disciples were always on the move, seeking new people with whom they could share the good news of the Messiah's arrival. It's much more comfortable to remain cloistered within our church walls, expecting "them" to come to "us," but it doesn't always work that way. Jesus' commission to us in Matthew 28:19–20 is for "us" to go to "them." We can do this while growing friendships in our everyday lives and incarnating Jesus as we go about our daily tasks. By the way, placing "community" after all the people groups in this list is not meant to label it as an afterthought or something to do if there is time left over. Jesus and His disciples spent the bulk of their time in the community, not in the synagogue. Ouch!

» **Yourself.** Learning our own likes and dislikes, strengths and weaknesses, and needs and choices will channel us to serve in ways consistent with how God created us. Building a relationship with oneself infers that we offer ourselves the same grace and respect that we offer others. When I began teaching as a young college graduate, my principal told my parents when they visited, "Cynthia is hardest on herself." We must prioritize the measures that enrich our spiritual, emotional, and physical health so we can be who God created us to be. The adage about putting on our own oxygen mask before placing it on our traveling companions applies to life on the ground as well.

Lest you feel burdened by the As and the Bs and want to scream, "I can't do it all!"—you're right! That's why we move on to the Cs and Ds. Keep reading. . . .

CREATE A LEADERSHIP TEAM

If you've ever considered going solo, drop that idea right now! Haven't you felt the weariness Moses experienced before his father-in-law educated him about sharing the burdens of leadership? Even Jesus chose a team to help carry out His mission. Not because He needed to, but He chose to.

If teamwork is not currently part of your church culture, you may be in a position to select your own team, board, or committee members. Or perhaps you have inherited a group of people who will work by your side. I have worked with teams of paid staff as well as groups of volunteer staff, and the principles remain the same for both. Choose people with strengths and points of view that vary from yours. The final decisions your team arrives at will be more thorough when resolved by folks with different perspectives. Look for people with abilities greater than your own—ministry is about the mission, not about who gets the credit.

The going wisdom at my former church was to select teammates who demonstrate character, competency, and chemistry. This was patterned after the selection process Bill Hybels helped establish at Willow Creek Community Church in South Barrington, Illinois. In *Courageous Leadership*, he describes character as based on a walk with Jesus that includes traits such as honesty, humility, trustworthiness, and a healthy work ethic. Competent people have excellent qualifications and can make valuable contributions to those they serve. Chemistry refers to enjoying one's relationship with fellow team members. That advice has served us well through the years. In *Children's Ministry That Works!*, Craig Jutila adds commitment and consistency to the original list of Cs.[3] Regardless of the qualifications you identify, building teamwork must be intentional. The work of growing relationships is ongoing but reaps great rewards.

DEFINE THE FOCUS

There's one more important thinking step before starting anything new or revamping the old. We need to define our focus and be exactly sure of

---

3   Craig Jutila, "Determining and Developing Your Leadership Team," in *Children's Ministry That Works!* (Loveland, CO: Group Publishing, 2002), 18–23.

what we are hoping to accomplish. We will flesh this out in chapter 2 when we discuss mission and vision, but for starters, it's important to remember that we are in the disciple-making business, not merely providing babysitting, entertaining, or character-building services.

Consider again the meaning of Jesus' words, "Go therefore and make disciples of all nations, baptizing them in the name of the Father and of the Son and of the Holy Spirit, teaching them to observe all that I have commanded you. And behold, I am with you always, to the end of the age" (Matthew 28:19–20). Jesus calls us to be disciple-makers, and He gives us the tools of Sacrament and Word. The Holy Spirit is the "disciple-Creator" as He instills faith in even a young child through water and Word in Baptism. Our role as parents and congregation is to nurture that faith as we continue to teach the Word. Some pastors clarify the congregational role very clearly in the Baptism ceremony. My pastors say, "I ask you as a congregation, do you promise to pray for the children in your midst, to provide for their Christian education so that they may learn about the God they have, and to model for them a godly life in both word and deed?" I love that question! Anyone sitting next to me in church would hear a resounding, "I do so promise!"

Older children who are not growing up in a Christian home come to faith in the same way, through Word and Sacrament. As we teach these children who Jesus is and why He came, the Spirit works in their hearts to receive the truth of God's Word. Baptism will serve as the "proof" that God has done His work to call each child to be His own. Growing into becoming a more faithful follower of Jesus begins on our watch and continues for a lifetime.

Being Jesus' disciple is more than intellectually knowing about Him. Throughout Jesus' life, the invitation He extended to various people in differing circumstances was "follow Me." Following Jesus is a very big deal because it entails all aspects of our life—how we live at home, how we treat others, what we think about, how we spend our time and use our resources, and how we arrive at decisions, to name just a few.

A word coined by David Csinos in *Children's Ministry That Fits* is "trans/formation." The author defines the root word *formation* as the process of being shaped by the Holy Spirit into the likeness of Christ.[4] The word *sanctification* is

---

4   David Csinos, *Children's Ministry That Fits* (Eugene, OR: Wipf & Stock, 2011), 19.

probably more familiar in our church tradition. "Now may the God of peace Himself sanctify you completely, and may your whole spirit and soul and body be kept blameless at the coming of our Lord Jesus Christ" (1 Thessalonians 5:23). Our desire is that our lives as well as the lives of our children reflect the qualities, or image, of Jesus. "For those whom He foreknew He also predestined to be conformed to the image of His Son" (Romans 8:29).

Transformation implies change. At our Baptism, our status with God dramatically changes from old to new, from death to life. And thankfully, God's work is not done. There are still fearful and doubting parts in all of us that need to be converted to greater faith and hope. As Paul writes, "Do not be conformed to this world, but be transformed by the renewal of your mind" (Romans 12:2). We are given the remarkable task of guiding children in this transformative process while we experience it ourselves.

Does life change occur through our own efforts or by following biblical examples of righteous people? Hardly! Sinful patterns still control parts of us that cannot be changed by our will or self-determination. As the Holy Spirit points out the sin that keeps us from reflecting Christ, He invites us toward repentance. He calls us to turn around and go in a different direction. The amazing thing is that what God asks of us, He also enables us to do! "And I am sure of this, that He who began a good work in you will bring it to completion at the day of Jesus Christ" (Philippians 1:6).

This is the foundation of our focus in working with children. Not simply giving them a fun place to come. Not simply helping them make friends. Not simply instilling in them good morals. Not simply teaching Bible facts. All these are good outcomes, but they are not the core of our mission. Our focus is to help grow disciples of Jesus whose lives reflect the Spirit within—lives of love, joy, peace, patience, kindness, goodness, faithfulness, gentleness, and self-control.

* * * *

I mingle with the parents on Sunday mornings, and if they're hanging out or visiting with one another during Sunday School, I try to enter into their conversations.

Janette Haak
Sheepfold Coordinator
St. Luke
Ann Arbor, MI

* * * *

In the past I have done surveys with ten questions asking parents' needs and/or desires for their child. I also like to have good communication with the Early Childhood Director, teachers in the school, and the school principal. These people are on the front lines and can give you great insight into the pulse of the families in your church and/or school.

Julie Burgess
Director of Family Life
St. Paul Lutheran Church and School
Ann Arbor, MI

* * * *

In order to effectively conduct a needs assessment, a sufficient amount of time in the organization is needed along with collaboration from staff members and volunteers from a variety of areas within the church. A variety of factors [must] be considered: socioeconomic statuses, common needs that they struggle to meet, and current resources on hand, resources that can be acquired through donation or grant funding. Once a comprehensive list of needs is created, a cost-benefit analysis of the various needs should be done, as well as a logic model to lay out the problem that needs to be addressed.

Kyle McCall
Graduate, Concordia University Texas
Austin, Texas

* * * *

It takes time but, because parents and children are there for you to have conversations with, it's well worth the effort to be visible at events and activities that don't necessarily involve your ministry area. Go to ballgames, participate in a Bible study or small group, or get involved in a community group (running club, book club, etc.). If you have a school connected with your church, walk the hallways before or after school starts to greet people, lead chapel, be a mystery reader for younger classes, and don't forget to build relationships with your teachers, pastors, and other staff.

Julie Burgess
Director of Family Life
St. Paul Lutheran Church and School
Ann Arbor, MI

* * * *

Checklist
for Church Assessments

Assess the Needs

» What is your first impression of the facility's exterior maintenance: building, grounds, parking lot, signage, etc.?

» What is your first impression of the facility's interior maintenance and decor: narthex, hallways, sanctuary, classrooms, bathrooms, signage, etc.?

» How enthusiastically does the congregation embrace children? Is the children's area attractive, age appropriate, clean, and up-to-date?

» What is the stated purpose of the church? How well does this serve as a guiding principle for various ministries?

» What is the discipleship process for adults and children?

» How does the church expect parents to spiritually influence their children?

» Do guests attend weekend worship services? If not, why? If so, how welcoming are the pastor and people? What follow-up is provided?

» Does the church membership reflect the makeup of the surrounding community? If not, what differences exist? Why?

» Anything else you observe?

Build Relationships

List the ways you intentionally build relationships with the following people groups. Do you see any areas in which God may be calling you to grow?

» Parents

» Children

» Volunteers

» Congregation

» Pastor, church leadership, boards

» Community

» Yourself

Create a Leadership Team

Write down the names of those who currently serve on your leadership team or those whom you believe would be an asset. Briefly describe the unique gifts each offers or could offer your group.

1.

2.

3.

4.

5.

6.

Define the Focus

» What is your ministry's current purpose statement?

» How would you explain what that means to a child?

» If your ministry does not have a formal statement, what do you believe are Jesus' deepest desires for the children who are or will be connected with your church?

Explain the Gospel Message to Children

The core message that God loves us and forgives us because of Jesus' death on our behalf must be shared with both Christian and non-Christian children. Here are several simple ways to explain this Good News story.

Idea 1: Personalize John 3:16 by inserting a person's name into the verse.

"For God so loved [Cynthia], that He gave His only Son, that [if Cynthia] believes in Him [Cynthia] should not perish but have eternal life" (John 3:16). What does this mean to you?

Idea 2: Use three *s* words—sin, separation, Savior—as a framework.

All people *sin,* and that wrongdoing *separates* us from God. We can't make our sin go away on our own. Because God loves us, He sacrificed His Son, Jesus, to be our *Savior.* When Jesus died on the cross, He took all our sins with Him and they died too. We receive God's gifts of forgiveness and life forever with Him. Does this Good News make sense to you?

Idea 3: Summarize the Gospel with colors. A small card with this explanation can be given to children along with colored beads on a safety pin, bracelet, or necklace.

The best friend that you can have is Jesus. He *always* loves you and He is *always* with you.

> » **Black bead:** You do and think things that don't match God's goodness. This is called sin, and it stands in the way of your friendship with God (Romans 3:23).

> » **White bead:** But God still loves you so much, and nothing you can do will make Him love you more (Jeremiah 31:3).

> » **Red bead:** Jesus came to die on the cross and take the punishment for your sins (Romans 5:8).

» **Blue bead:** Faith is knowing that your friendship with Jesus is because of what He did for you. This gift of faith is given by the Holy Spirit when you hear God's Word and are baptized as His child (Romans 6:4).

» **Green bead:** God wants your friendship with Him to be alive and grow. You can get to know Him better when you read His Word, pray to Him, worship Him, and talk about Him with other people (2 Peter 3:18).

» **Yellow bead:** You can spend the rest of your life with your best friend Jesus now and when you live with Him in heaven (Revelation 2:10).

If you know this is true, you can talk to Him like this:

Dear Jesus, thank You for Your big love for me. Forgive me for all the wrong things I have done. Thank You for taking my sins away when You died on the cross. Help me to grow in knowing You and to share this Good News with others. Amen.

If you're not sure, you can talk with Him like this:

Dear Jesus, please keep showing me who You are and what You have done for me. Amen.

Who's My Target Audience?

"Tell to the coming generation the glorious deeds of the Lord, and His might, and the wonders that He has done. He . . . commanded our fathers to teach to their children, that the next generation might know them, the children yet unborn, and arise and tell them to their children, so that they should set their hope in God and not forget the works of God, but keep His commandments." Psalm 78:4–7

When I was invited to move from Sunday School superintendent to children's ministry director at our church, no job description was given. So I decided to go to the top and see what the Scriptures had to say about my role. Years ago, my husband had given me a Bible reference tool that became very useful for this project. When a word is typed and entered into the tool, each Scripture verse mentioning that word is identified one at a time. I typed "children," "church," "teacher," "parents," "mother," and "father" and read all the verses in which those words were used. That was quite an undertaking. To my dismay, no job description for children's ministry director surfaced. In fact, I couldn't even find clues for how the congregation was to relate to children. But what I did discover was God's intent for *parents* to teach their children about Him.

Now what? I had equipped many Sunday School teachers to instruct children, and my new role would require supervising even more programs that didn't involve parents—midweek classes, VBS, sports, childcare, special events, and so on. In light of this new biblical information, what was I to do?

And if that wasn't enough to gain my attention, I noticed that conferences for children's ministry were now adding topics focused on parents serving as the primary faith-nurturers of their children. Calling it a "new concept" wasn't quite accurate, for had I not just discovered that truth in Scripture? In addition, doesn't each section of Luther's Small Catechism begin with the words: "As the head of the family should teach it in a simple way to his household"? Folks in Luther's day never considered that the church would hold classes for their children. Perhaps the concept of parents' spiritual responsibilities was only "new" to us in the twenty-first century.

As we look back on history, a shift has taken place in our thinking. Somewhere along the line, the responsibility for teaching spiritual truths to children was removed from the laps of parents and handed over to "professionals." And I was one of those "professionals" who had just had an about-face! My immediate audience was not necessarily the children but the parents who care for their children.

No, we didn't chuck all our programs. Some families are simply not positioned to be faith-forming centers all on their own. But we did take a good look at how we could involve parents in preexisting programs, and we initiated ways we could help them realize and rediscover their God-given roles. Deuteronomy 6:6–9 took on new meaning:

> And these words that I command you today shall be on your heart. You shall teach them diligently to your children, and shall talk of them when you sit in your house, and when you walk by the way, and when you lie down, and when you rise. You shall bind them as a sign on your hand, and they shall be as frontlets between your eyes. You shall write them on the doorposts of your house and on your gates.

Because of Scripture passages such as these, our target audience changed from only children to include parents—parents who would serve as partners with us, spiritually teaching the children together.

Ben Freudenburg, author of *The Family Friendly Church* and director of the Concordia Center for the Family at Concordia University Ann Arbor, describes the old paradigm of children's ministry as "church-centered, home-supported" and illustrates that concept using a drawing of a church surrounded by homes with arrows pointing inward toward the church. His description of the newer concept as "home-centered, church-supported" is illustrated with the same depiction of buildings, but the arrows are now pointing outward from the church toward the homes.[5] This paradigm shift is what my team and I wanted to emphasize because it more closely aligned with God's perspective and how we, as Lutherans, have understood children's ministry since the writing of the Small Catechism.

For starters, we reevaluated the basic tenets of our ministry. We added "family-focused" to our list of values. We reformatted the take-home papers given to children after Sunday School and initiated a parent newsletter. "Partnering with parents" now preceded the mission statement. These small changes helped focus all of us on our primary target audience: the parents.

I once saw a picture of a candy jar filled with 168 pieces of candy. All were one color with the exception of 2 pieces. This illustration depicted the 168 hours in the week. If parents rely on the two hours of church and Sunday School as their only means of spiritual nurture for their children, they are missing 166 other hours of opportunity. After creating my own candy jar to use as an illustration, my husband suggested that including the hours for sleep might not be a fair depiction, so now my candy jar has 2 red pieces and 112 yellow pieces. The image still makes the point.

There is much work to do. Some Christian parents have failed to fully grasp God's vision for their role as parents, and an even bigger gap exists between a parent who applies Deuteronomy 6 and one who is not even conscious of spiritual and biblical realities. How can we help bridge these gaps by inviting people to find God's Word compelling enough to make changes in their lives?

Let's begin by taking time to reflect on the unique settings in our churches and communities through which God works to grow His kingdom.

---

5   Ben Freudenburg, *The Family Friendly Church* (Loveland: Group Publishing, 1998).

What's Our Paradigm?

Read chapter 1. Gather with your team and discuss the following questions.

1. How do the leaders, volunteers, and parents in your congregation demonstrate that they believe the church is responsible for the spiritual training of the children?

2. How do the leaders, volunteers, and parents in your congregation demonstrate that they believe parents are responsible for the spiritual training of the children?

3. Read Deuteronomy 6:4–9. How does your church teach these principles to parents?

4. What is the relationship between your church and your members' homes? Are you primarily church-centered, home-supported or home-centered, church-supported?

5. Is there willingness to more fully embrace the second paradigm?

Where Shall We Go?

"Where there is no prophetic vision the people cast off restraint."
Proverbs 29:18

"When the Spirit of truth comes, He will guide you into all the
truth, for He will not speak on His own authority, but whatever
He hears He will speak, and He will declare to you the things
that are to come." John 16:13

Vision, purpose, mission, goals—we throw these words around, and confusion abounds. Their meanings seem to blur into one another. We may even question their appropriateness in the church setting and wonder whether language suited to the business world is tainting the church. The bottom line, however, is asking this: Who does God want us to be? And what is He planning for us to do in this next season of ministry at the place He has called us to serve? We carry out this work not to bring glory to ourselves but to bring glory to Him, so we go to Him and to His Word for answers to these important questions.

Whether you lead one program for children or oversee the entire children's ministry, the exercise of pursuing answers to the above questions will prove worthwhile. Just keep in mind that the vision/purpose/mission you and your team develop for the children must support the broader vision/purpose/mission of the church at large. If your church's existing statement is stated simply and clearly, you may choose to use the same words to reflect the children's ministry. Even so, I challenge you to carefully consider how you will practically live it out as you guide the children.

Searching online for the first four words in this chapter would surface a variety of definitions. Allow me to share my own brief descriptions. My students find it helpful to hear examples in the context of some of my own hobbies. This paves the way for them to apply these concepts to the more abstract context of faith. I'll use the example of gardening to attempt to clarify these muddy waters.

VISION

The driving question behind defining one's vision is "where": Where do you want to go?

I love to garden. In my yard, I envision a colorful and well-manicured park-like setting that displays God's beauty as reflected in His creation. This is the end result, the mental picture that inspires me to keep plugging along even when critters get voracious or muscles get cranky.

As we transition our thoughts to the church setting, think ahead and toward the future. What faith-filled picture can you envision for the future of your ministry? What is your desired outcome? When all is said and done, what do you hope to see? Don't let my use of the word *what* in these questions throw you off. They press toward the future, where you want to go. Write down anything that pops in your head, and return to your notes at various intervals. Be patient—this process takes time to unfold.

A beautiful example of vision is Martin Luther King's "I Have a Dream" speech, which still motivates people more than fifty years after it was given. His mind's eye looked toward the future as he proclaimed, "I have a dream that my four little children will one day live in a nation where they will not be judged by the color of their skin but by the content of their character." We still work toward that dream.

Jesus knew that His life extended beyond what He experienced on this earth. He looked beyond the present and into the future when He told His disciples, "I know where I came from and where I am going" (John 8:14). His vision of an eternal relationship with us kept Him faithful during His most difficult days on this earth.

PURPOSE

The driving question behind defining one's purpose is "why": Why does your ministry exist?

To return to our gardening illustration, my purpose in working in my yard is to nurture the beauty of God's creation. Another gardener may have purpose different from mine, and that is perfectly fine. Just as individuals differ, churches and ministries within those churches differ, even though we share commonalities.

Go deep to the heart of the answer to the question of "why." Jot down everything that comes to mind. Many things will initially surface; your list may include ideas like teaching the Bible, attracting new families, or helping parents guide their children. But don't stop there. *Why* do you want to do these things? If you press toward answering this question, you will ultimately come to the core truth, which has something to do with knowing God and His love in Jesus Christ. Keep writing down your thoughts. Search Scripture to gain a clear understanding of Jesus' purpose. Clarity will come through this prayerful process, but keep in mind that it will unfold at God's pace, not your own.

MISSION

The driving question behind defining one's mission is "what": What is the task at hand? What work are you and your team supposed to do?

Let's return to my yard. My mission is to spend time working in my flower and vegetable gardens. That's the task at hand when I don my old clothes, sun hat, and gloves.

Because mission and purpose are closely related, many churches use these terms synonymously. If you look at some churches' mission/purpose statements, they may answer why and what at the same time. That's perfectly fine and may be where you end up as well. The intent is not to quibble over identifying exactly what kind of statement you have produced. I am breaking down these definitions to press your mind toward thinking deeply about these issues. So for the time being, refocus on what God is inviting you and your team to do at this point in time, and put your thoughts on paper or screen.

Jesus' mission is described in several ways. Luke 4:18–19 quotes Isaiah: "To proclaim good news to the poor . . . to proclaim liberty to the captives and recovering of sight to the blind, to set at liberty those who are oppressed, to proclaim the year of the Lord's favor." In Luke 19:10, we read that He came "to seek and to save the lost." And in John 18:37, He tells Pilate, "For this purpose I was born and for this purpose I have come into the world—to bear witness to the truth." As believers in Christ, who is the truth, we can pray that the Holy Spirit will guide our mission to look like His.

GOALS

The driving question behind defining one's goals is "how": How will all this come about? How will you live out your purpose, complete your mission, and move toward your vision? Your goals will help you accomplish this.

During the growing season, my gardening goals include trimming shrubs, planting flowers and vegetables, watering and fertilizing, killing weeds and bugs, edging beds, and deadheading spent flowers. When some tasks get crossed off the list, new ones arise.

Goals are the steps or tasks needed to carry out the vision, purpose, and mission—those duties you need to complete to get the job done. Without goals or objectives, you are left with abstract ideas. Goals are not static; they can change each year or season, or they can differ for each program. When your goals are accomplished, more can be created.

Note that we started with the where, why, and what questions. "How" must be the *last* question we ask. We usually want to start doing new things before we think through the reasons for doing them. If these questions are taken out of order, all the programs and classes you offer may have nothing to do with the deeper purpose to which you have been called. Trust me; the practical will follow if the foundation is in place.

TYING IT ALL TOGETHER

Don't get hung up on semantics. As I mentioned earlier, sometimes terms are used interchangeably. Some churches create one statement that combines their vision, purpose, and mission. Others create multiple statements to reflect each facet individually. There is no right or wrong. Vision/purpose/mission (V/P/M) statements are not end-all solutions—they are tools. What *is* important is to focus all of this on God's will, as revealed in His Word. He promises to work through You according to His plan (Ephesian 2:8–10). Pray that you are open to where God is leading and that you seek clarity from Him as to why He placed the people in your particular church at your particular location at this particular time in history. And of equal importance is actually using the statement you have created. How sad to spend time with the process only to shelve it and ignore its ability to set a course and clarify decisions that need to be made.

Seeking answers to these questions is hard, prayerful work. We trust God's promise when He says, "I will instruct you and teach you in the way you should go; I will counsel you" (Psalm 32:8). Clarity can come in a variety of ways—in light of Scripture and through the guidance of the Holy Spirit, our V/P/M can become well-defined when we hear a story, observe what someone else doing, or simply see a need. It may come quickly like an epiphany or more slowly, piece by piece. But however it comes, it will be according to God's timing and not humanly imposed. This work is about God's intent, not ours. Patiently and prayerfully take your time with the process.

Bill Hybels suggested during Willow Creek's 2007 Leadership Summit that there are two approaches to clarifying vision. The first approach involves one leader spending time alone with God in His Word for wisdom with these questions. The second invites key leaders to take a role in prayerfully working through these questions as a team—again, in light of God's Word and praying for His will to be done. This may be a less efficient use of time, but it builds community and increases ownership, two important factors needed to move forward.

Once the V/P/M and goals are defined, you may experience a passion and energy to work; you may even sense that you were born for this moment in time. Remember Mordecai's great appeal to Esther? "And who knows whether you have not come to the kingdom for such a time as this?" (Esther 4:14). Your excitement will also fuel your volunteers. There's nothing worse than slugging in the trenches without knowing why you're working so hard. It's like trying to get through a tough college class and forgetting why you're even in school. But when we focus on a deeper purpose and thank God for the children who will hear about His love and forgiveness, even routine tasks such as sharpening pencils or rearranging classrooms can take on new meaning.

Once your V/P/M is developed, casting it to the entire church is critical. Spread the word through as many avenues as possible. Discuss it in meetings, write about it in memos, include it in newsletters, and mention it in formal and informal conversations. Repeat, repeat, repeat—ideas need to be heard many times for them to sink in. Be creative—a sentence here, a paragraph there, two minutes in the middle of a meeting, a reference in a talk. At my former church, even though the mission was painted on the arches entering the children's area, I was always taken aback when volunteers still couldn't remember those words that were so prominently displayed. Keep communicating!

Knowing your V/P/M will be invaluable for the future of your ministry. It will enhance cooperation between volunteers who serve in different capacities, bringing them together under one benchmark and moving them forward in one direction. It will provide the glue between individual programs and events, unifying their objectives. When you create a new program or tweak an existing one, you can now resolve to fulfill the deeper purpose that was established. When you evaluate an event upon its completion, you can know whether your goals have been accomplished.

Finally, let me mention one more thing—values. Values are one-word characteristics that are the most important tenets within your ministry. They are guideposts that can focus you and your team. Like those bumpers children use in bowling, they can help you stay on course. For example, these are the values that we developed in my previous church: Bible-based, secure, creative, nurturing, relevant, family-focused, prayerful. Any program idea that did not fit those parameters was discarded, and all the projects we did undertake had to connect with all seven values. You may want to experiment with this suggestion and brainstorm some words with your team. If several poignant terms rise to the surface, see if they can serve as "bumpers" to help your team reach its target.

Flowchart to Develop the Vision Process

Vision	Purpose	Mission	Goals	Values
Where do you want to go?	**Why** does your ministry exist?	**What** are you supposed to do?	**How** will all this come about?	**What** are your guiding principles?
Brainstorm all thoughts	Brainstorm all thoughts	Brainstorm all thoughts	Brainstorm all thoughts	Brainstorm all thoughts
Sample statements	Sample statements	Sample statements	Sample statements	Sample words or phrases
Our clearest summary so far	Our clearest summary so far	Our clearest summary so far	Our clearest summary so far	Our clearest summary so far

With a prayer that God will work through us in this time and place according to His will, this is the verbiage we will present to the congregation:

Chapter 3

How Could Children's Ministry Look at My Church?

"Ask, and it will be given to you; seek, and you will find; knock, and it will be opened to you. For everyone who asks receives, and the one who seeks finds, and to the one who knocks it will be opened." Matthew 7:7–8

When I was growing up, the phrase "children's ministry" didn't exist. My church did have a Sunday School and a parochial school, both of which my siblings and I attended. If our family visited Grandma Kiehl in Missouri during the summer, we went to her Vacation Bible School with our cousins. While recently sorting through some keepsakes in my basement, I found a few crafts preserved from that special summer experience. But "children's ministry"? No one would have known what we were talking about!

Perhaps children's ministry at your church looks very much like it did back in the day—one or two simple programs. Or perhaps new opportunities have sprung up along the way and more options for kids exist. But one thing most of us have in common is that we still provide Sunday Schools.

SUNDAY SCHOOL

Involving children in church has taken on many forms throughout history. Sunday School began back in the 1780s in Great Britain with one man's effort to free children living in slums from a life of poverty, illiteracy, and crime. Over the next two hundred years, it morphed into teaching the Bible to children primarily from our congregations. What is the purpose of Sunday School in your congregation today? Now that you have clarified your V/P/M, you will want to ask how your Sunday School carries out this single-minded cause that you have placed front and center for your ministry.

Sunday Schools usually adopt one of three formats. The most familiar is the traditional classroom where the teacher covers all aspects of each lesson. This plan is appealing because of its familiarity and because it requires fewer teachers to lead it. Another option many churches have adopted is the large-group to small-group format. Children gather in a large group for music and the Bible presentation and then follow up in smaller clusters for discussion and Bible learning activities. While requiring more staff, teachers have more focused job descriptions that enable them to serve in their areas of strength rather than having to be all things to all people. A third possibility is the rotation model, where children can either move to several stations each week or rotate each week to a different station. Volunteers prepare their portion of the lesson and repeat it with each group that comes to their location. Many VBS curricula have adopted this format in recent years.

Most of us pick up a curriculum and teach it without considering how a Christian educational model can best influence the faith formation of the children. The authors of *Perspectives on Children's Spiritual Formation* offer four different philosophies[6] of how they believe children are spiritually formed:

1. The Contemplative-Reflective approach encourages personal contact with God through prayer and quiet reflection.

2. A systematic study of God's Word that focuses on Bible memorization uses the Instructional-Analytic approach.

3. Focusing on practical Bible application through numerous Bible activities describes the Pragmatic-Participatory approach.

---

6 Michael Anthony, ed., *Perspectives on Children's Spiritual Formation* (Nashville: Broadman & Holman, 2006).

4. And finally, a high-energy model with instructional technology is the Media-Driven Active-Engagement approach. Considering these four philosophies challenges us to identify the elements we want to incorporate in our Sunday School to enable children to grow more Christlike. Carefully studying and choosing options enables us to make deliberate decisions that support our ministry goals.

NURSERY AND CRY ROOM

Does your church have a nursery or cry room? Whether the nursery is staffed by volunteers or whether the cry room is simply available for parents to bring their fussy little ones during the service, maintaining this space can be considered a function of children's ministry. Tasks such as routine cleaning, refreshing decor, and updating toys are most appreciated by parents who want their children to experience a safe and pleasant environment.

It is important for volunteers who may serve in this area to see their service not as simple babysitting, but rather as ministry to the littlest ones, sharing Jesus' love with His precious children as they build that important foundation of trust. Their service also benefits the parents, allowing them to worship freely and showing them that the church loves and cares for their treasured infants and toddlers. Find ways to communicate that this room is not viewed as a substitute for church—we love to have children worshiping with us—but as another way for families to learn of Jesus and His love.

WORSHIP SERVICES

Even though the worship service is not a program itself, sustaining the involvement of children can be one aspect of children's ministry. Some churches simply take the presence of children for granted. Others support parents' efforts to teach their own children to attend church by providing children's worship bulletins or children's messages. Still others offer Sunday School or children's worship at the same time as adult worship.

I once attended a church where the pastor actually stopped his sermon and told the congregation he would wait for me to leave the sanctuary with my baby, who had let out a sudden squawk. Hopefully this would not take place in your church! Work with the leaders of your own church to prayerfully define the role of children in the worship services. I can only imagine scenarios of Jesus with outstretched and welcoming arms.

VACATION BIBLE SCHOOL

Most Lutheran churches also have summer Vacation Bible School. From the church's perspective, the purpose of most VBS programs is to reach out to unchurched kids. However, our informal surveys have shown that VBS can be populated primarily by church families and by parents who bring their children to programs at various churches during the summer, craving a respite while their children enjoy constructive activities in a safe environment at no or low cost. Take the time to carefully look at the children who attend your program to discern whether you are meeting your goals.

VBS takes a lot of work! As a result, many large nondenominational churches have actually stepped away from this program, focusing their energy instead on providing quality Sunday programs. Those congregations that still want to offer a summer extracurricular activity may take their kids to camp or pay for an outside group to come in and lead VBS, both at a much greater expense to families.

This shift opens the door for our Lutheran churches to step into the void and offer a wonderful summer VBS experience for neighborhood kids. Actually reaching unchurched kids will require creative publicity, but it can be done. Going one step further and offering a quality closing performance and ice-cream social in the evening for families can give parents, grandparents, and friends an opportunity to experience your church's culture firsthand.

PRESCHOOL AND DAY SCHOOL

Perhaps your church sponsors a preschool or hosts a parochial school on the premises. Churches that support parochial education hold fast to the desire to give children a Christian foundation in all aspects of life.

The percentage of non-Lutheran and even non-Christian children attending parochial schools has increased over the years. This provides a mission field right at our back door. Even if the preschool or Day School is not officially placed under the umbrella of children's ministry at your church, both directly relate to your mission. Your role as a leader in children's ministry can help facilitate inviting families to participate in the faith life of the congregation. It is true that churches that do not have parochial schools probably have additional resources to offer more elaborate events for children and families. But if God has called your church to financially invest in this mission, make the most of this opportunity.

Our church sponsors a preschool and looks for ways to invite the families to join church activities. We recently hosted a free pizza and game night for families. Ninety percent of our church and preschool families attended. What joy we experienced watching the families mingle and have fun with one another! In addition, the preschool and Sunday School children joined together to sing during an Advent service and on a Sunday morning. Unchurched preschool families are inviting their friends to sign up for our summer VBS. Partnership takes deliberate effort, but it can be done!

SPECIAL-NEEDS SUPPORT

During my first years of teaching, I was friends with a woman who happened to be deaf. She was part of a deaf community who rarely attended church. Few opportunities existed at the time for them to understand and participate.

I heard the same report from parents whose children attended our church's friendship class for young people with cognitive, emotional, and physical needs. These parents shared stories of friends who could not find churches because the congregation was unprepared to handle their unique circumstances. These moms and dads welcomed a place that loved their children just as they were. They appreciated the one-hour break to attend the worship service knowing that their children were in a safe and Jesus-centered environment.

Churches that take the time to understand and try to support parents who live with children with Down syndrome, communication disorders, physical limitations, autism spectrum disorder, or learning disabilities have a unique call in God's kingdom. Entire family systems are affected by these diagnoses. Discipleship opportunities abound when parents question why God would allow their dreams to shatter. Congregational attitudes can be softened as we reach out with Jesus' love to those different from ourselves. But in reality, because we live in a broken world, we all have special needs; some of ours are on the inside and well hidden from people, while others are quite visible on the outside.

If God calls your church to work with this people group, contact other churches that have a well-established special-needs ministry for guidance. Hearing about their successes and failures will guide your own preparations.

BAPTISM AND CRADLE ROLL

Because of our theology of Baptism, your church may have a cradle roll, a term that has been around for years. It may simply be defined as a list of children who have been baptized during the past year, or it may be as extensive as providing resources and home visits for new parents. What would you like your cradle roll or Baptism ministry to look like at your church? A brainstorming session with your pastor may produce some surprising and creative results.

Baptism offers a perfect opportunity to help parents understand God's perspective on their role. If we want to partner with parents to raise their children in the Christian faith, what better time to start than at the beginning of their child's life? If your church does not offer a class for parents seeking Baptism for their children, this could be a prime time to consider doing so.

The class could begin with a description of our church body's refreshing teaching on Baptism. What a gift to know that in our inability to come to God, He reaches down to us to call us His own! Parents will hear that they and their child are created, redeemed, and filled by God Himself when His name is placed on them in Baptism. In my experience, many parents who request Baptism for their child have not been faithful in their own church attendance. This time together spent in preparation can enhance their return to the community life of the church.

Another aspect of the class could be practical ideas on how to lay that foundation of prayer, talking about God (or "God talk"), Bible time, and blessing in the home. Those who did not experience these devotional activities during their own childhoods may not be aware of the possibilities with their own children. You have the opportunity to change the course of countless children's lives at home!

STEPPING-STONE EVENTS

Additional events that focus on the home, called stepping stones or milestones, have been used in churches in more recent years. The foundational idea behind this concept is to use a child's natural maturation stages as opportunities to partner with their parents to spiritually guide the children. Some churches purchase a curriculum to use and follow. Others explore various programs for ideas and then create their own events. Be sure to consider the needs of your own faith community, the time required to create these events, and the availability of leadership to actually make them happen. You will have to prayerfully decide if that person is you.

Stepping-stone events usually bring parents and their children together at the same time. Focusing on a target audience composed of both children and parents can be challenging but not impossible with creative preparation. You may already be familiar with bringing third graders and their parents together to teach them how to use the Bible. It can be done!

Baptism is usually the first stepping stone. Parents may choose to bring their infants, but since parents are the target audience for this particular topic, it would be best to have babysitting available for the stepping-stone event itself. Perhaps you have heard of congregations creating faith chests to give to children when they are baptized. That concept originated from the stepping-stone/milestone model. The chest provides a place where children can keep the special mementos they receive through the years. As children mature, churches can create additional experiences to guide them and their parents to grow in their faith. These occasions may be carried out throughout a child's elementary years, or by partnering with the youth ministry, they could continue all the way through high school graduation. How often churches provide these events varies greatly.

An important component is giving parents a spiritual tool to use later at home with their children. For example, if you want to teach young families about home devotions, you could give your preschoolers a picture Bible. If you want to teach parents how to pray with their children, a prayer booklet could help them continue the practice at home. Be creative in looking for ways to encourage additional spiritual habits, such as God talk or giving a blessing or helping children serve others.

Upon completion of a stepping-stone or milestone event, families are often recognized in front of the congregation. The pastor invites the children and their parents to come forward to the Communion rail and receive a commission or a blessing. If appropriate, a gift could be given at this time (such as a Bible). This public step once again highlights parents as the primary faith-nurturers of their children.

PARENTING CLASSES

Parenting classes can serve as an alternative or supplement to stepping stones. A class could be designed as a stand-alone session on a particular topic or as a series of classes. Once again, curricula are available, or a creative individual could create his or her own course. You may observe a need for basic parenting skills, such as providing discipline or having fun with their kids. Parents may benefit from learning how to create Christian traditions in their homes. If creating stepping-stone events is too demanding at the moment, you may want to design a class that addresses the same topics such as prayer, God talk, home devotions, or blessing children. The possibilities to walk beside parents as they raise their children are unlimited.

COMMUNITY FAMILY EVENTS

Parents often look for fun and affordable family events throughout the year to enjoy with their children. Many churches create occasions that make it easy for kids to invite classmates or for families to invite neighbors and friends. Some people call these "seeker" events—happenings that those who are unchurched or not yet Christians can still feel comfortable attending. And because they are sponsored by churches rather than community organizations, you have the opportunity to share the Gospel story with those who attend. The message of Jesus' forgiving love can be proclaimed through a puppet show at a Christmas extravaganza, a Journey to the Cross event at an Easter fair, or booklets given at a block party.

An entire congregation can rally behind these events designed to welcome friends and neighbors. Look for ways your faith community can build relationships with new folks who attend. Friendships with God's people can open doors for others to be receptive to hearing about our Savior.

MANY MORE POSSIBILITIES

The unique setting of your church and its surrounding neighborhood community will and should influence the types of programs you consider for children and families. For example, "Divorce Care for Kids" can be offered for children or to supplement courses for single parents. A "Parents Night Out for Respite Care" can help support moms and dads who need a break from the unique and exhausting challenges they face every day in their homes with children with special needs. If your community places a high value on athletics, a sports ministry may be a way to connect with children. Preschools can augment their program with daytime childcare, story time for toddlers, or playdates for preschoolers and their moms. The list is endless: MOPS (Mothers of Preschoolers), home school support, after-school programs, music lessons, programs to earn religious badges for clubs. Look at the people within and surrounding your church, and ask God to open your eyes to opportunities to speak into their lives with His message of hope.

However, I must offer a warning. Our purpose is *not* to fill up your church calendar with more and more events, equating more activities with deeper faith. Willow Creek's REVEAL survey knocked down that fallacy very quickly. Events and activities hosted by a church may have nothing to do with nurturing faith. That is why your motivation and subsequent choices are critical. What do you want to accomplish by hosting a particular event or class? Is it tied to the vision and mission for your children's ministry? Pray for God's guidance and serve confidently in the work set before you.

Offering evening weekday classes for children and adults might be one more thing to complicate their already busy schedules, or they might be a critical tool to mature the faith of people of all ages. Offering a children's choir might place your weary parents behind the wheel one more night a week, or choir might be a beautiful way to teach children to worship God. Creating a family event for Christmas or Easter might simply add one more fun activity on the family holiday calendar, or with deliberation, it could completely change how families understand those holy days.

Prayerfully examine your motives, and prioritize God's best for your church. You have probably heard the saying "The good is the enemy of the best." This applies to the church calendar as well. Heed its message, and learn to say no to all those good ideas that could prevent you from saying yes to

God's better call for you and your faith community as you reach out to your neighbors with God's saving Word. Focus on the vision and mission that your congregation has in place to keep from getting distracted with the "good."

* * * *

We changed Sunday School this year to make it more interactive, energetic, and fun. We call it "Christ Connections." We begin with a ten-minute high-energy opening of songs, skits, puppets, etc. . . . followed by a twenty-minute in-depth, age-appropriate, activity-based lesson. After that there is a twenty-minute all-group fun activity— it is different every week, and the kids are now *participating* in the Bible learning. One little girl recently wrote down a prayer request during worship and handed it in. It said, "I wish Christ Connections was longer each week." This totally made my week and made me realize the effort to improve was worth it!

Dave Wright
Family Life Director
Our Savior Lutheran Church and School
Lansing, MI

* * * *

Leadership Team Activity to Select Programs for Your Church

Directions: Enlarge, print, and cut out the following program ideas. Add additional thoughts that people suggested your church implement. Set aside a time period that will not be rushed. As a group, select the most important possibilities that best carry out the vision/purpose/mission that you have clarified for your ministry. Continue the selection process until you have arrived at the choices that are workable for your team during the next phase of ministry.

Alternative suggestion: Print out a set of cards for each individual. Allow time for each person to select the top five means each believes best carries out the vision/purpose/mission you have clarified for your ministry. Ask each person to explain his or her rationale. As a group, narrow down the selections to what would work for your team during the next phase of ministry.

Sunday School	Respite Care for Parents
Nursery	Sports Ministry
Cry Room	Music Lessons
Vacation Bible School	After-School Programs
Preschool	MOPS
Daytime Childcare	Home School Support
Toddler Story Time	Scout Awards
Parents and Twos	Family Christmas Event
Toddler Playdates	Easter Family Event
Day School	Fall Family Event
Baptism Class for Parents	Parenting Classes
Cradle Roll	Family Movie Night
Stepping-Stone Events	Babysitting for Parent's Night Out
Kids Choir	Church Picnic
Weekday Classes	Family Christmas Caroling
Divorce Care for Kids	Special-Needs Classes

Steps to Set Up or Reinvent a Sunday School

1. Prayerful foundation
   - Meet with team to clarify vision, purpose, and mission
   - Meet with church leadership to cast vision
   - Clarify source and availability of financial resources

2. Philosophy and format
   - Decide format—traditional classes, large group to small group, rotation model
   - Clarify teaching necessities to promote life change in the children
   - Determine family involvement
   - Decide how to group children—by age, mixed, or gender
   - Establish day's schedule
   - Calendarize the Sunday School year

3. Curriculum
   - Identify what is important to teach
   - How long to stay on one topic
   - Same or different lessons for all ages of children
   - Music, games, crafts, and snacks support day's theme
   - Availability of parent take-homes
   - Make the purchase

4. Policies and procedures
   - Explore safety concerns
   - Set teacher-to-student ratio

- Identify snack/food allergies
- Establish discipline protocols
- Prepare policy manual and applications

5. Volunteers
   - Prepare job descriptions
   - Recruit volunteers
   - Create substitute list
   - Screen staff
   - Train volunteers—get them acquainted with curriculum
   - Train volunteers in policies
   - Give policy manuals and job descriptions
   - Process applications

6. Facilities
   - Gather or purchase supplies (paper, pencils, Bibles, arts/crafts, cleaning, snacks, etc.)
   - Reserve classrooms
   - Prepare rooms and furnishings for learning

7. Advertise the new Sunday School
   - Church members
   - Church friends
   - Community

8. Prayerfully receive feedback
   - Children
   - Parents
   - Teachers

Chapter 4

How Can We Transition toward Growing Faith in Our Homes?

"You shall teach them to your children, talking of them when you are sitting in your house, and when you are walking by the way, and when you lie down, and when you rise. You shall write them on the doorposts of your house and on your gates, that your days and the days of your children may be multiplied in the land that the LORD swore to your fathers to give them, as long as the heavens are above the earth." Deuteronomy 11:19–21

My husband plays and teaches the bagpipes. Many students have walked through our front door with chanter and pipes in hand. Some of the sounds emanating from our basement make me cringe; others put a smile on my face. Regardless of any perceptive listening skills, there is no way I could take the place of my husband and teach those students how to play grace notes or how to march, blow, finger notes, squeeze their arm, keep their drones steady, and recall the music all at the same time. We can't teach others what we don't experience ourselves.

The same holds true with helping our children recognize God's love in their lives and trusting that He will use His Word to lead His disciples into all truth. Parents who do not focus on their own faith lives will be unable to engage their children spiritually as Moses directed them to do in the Deuteronomy passage listed above. We can ask parents to do all the "right things"—pray, lead devotions, talk about God—but if these do not come from a heart of personally knowing and loving Him, these practices will be short-lived at best. Our mission to build children into disciples is accompanied by the mission to develop their parents into Christ-followers as well. Only then will they be able to see God's will for them to lead their children in the ways of Christ.

Even in the homes of committed Christians, faithfully and consistently leading our children spiritually is challenging. Why should we be surprised? The one who does not want Christ to be preeminent is doing his best to thwart any efforts toward that end. He fills our minds with excuses: I don't have the time. There's so much going on. I'm tired. I'll get to it tomorrow. My kids won't listen. I don't know what to do. I didn't have an example growing up. And on and on and on. Dr. Timothy Paul Jones says that the two biggest blocks for parents boil down to time and training.[7]

TIME

There is no denying that life is busy with children in our homes. Between the time devoted to meeting their needs, extended family demands, maintaining our homes and possessions, work, volunteer tasks, and social engagements, our calendars fill up very quickly. Urgent demands take precedence over important ongoing responsibilities.

I love the familiar rock-and-sand illustration Stephen Covey used to help us understand priorities.[8] The only way to fill a jar with sand and rocks of various sizes is to start with the biggest rocks and finish with pouring in the sand, which will seep into all the nooks and crannies.

We often live our lives in the reverse sequence, filling our hours with inconsequential tasks (sand) that allow no room for bigger essentials (biggest rocks). "Seek first the kingdom of God and His righteousness, and all these things will be added to you" (Mathew 6:33). When we grasp the significance of the eternal, we are freer to let go of the lesser things that occupy our minds and our time.

---

7   T. P. Jones, *Family Ministry Field Guide* (Indianapolis: Wesleyan Publishing House, 2011).

8   Stephen Covey, *7 Habits of Highly Effective People* (New York: Simon & Schuster, 1990).

TRAINING

Activities that were part of our own growing-up years are easily incorporated into the rhythms of our own homes when it is our turn to parent, assuming that these actions stir up pleasant memories. If we experienced practices such as prayer, Bible reading, family devotions, family nights, or God talk, it seems natural to share these rituals with our children. For someone new to these concepts, the above inventory can be a long and intimidating laundry list of formalities. Having a trainer walk side by side with them may be just what some parents need. Trainers offer much needed encouragement and motivation in other areas of life—why not in spiritual arenas as well?

Unfortunately, an exercise routine has not been a priority most of my life. Recognizing my own lack of initiation in this area, I eventually hired a trainer to push me to build muscle and strengthen my core. My husband and I also made water aerobics part of our morning routine three days a week. This accountability enables us remain faithful to those practices that benefit our bodies.

Church leaders can serve as trainers for parents needing to develop spiritual habits at home. They, like my coaches, must start with holding out the vision of why change is desired. Then they create and oversee manageable routines that build upon previous success. A heavy dose of encouragement on sluggish days keeps the momentum going. What a God-given privilege to guide parents to guide their children spiritually!

STEP 1—CLARIFY THE "WHY"

Parents can feel that they are in a losing battle to the culture when it comes to influencing their children. But despite common perceptions, Barna Research shows that parents are the main faith-influencers of their children. Simply hearing this fact encourages parents to persevere. In addition, stories of other parents' attempts to nurture faith at home as well as stories of kids whose parents' efforts have made a difference offer further motivation.

Timothy Paul Jones writes in a very thought-provoking manner that most parents recognize the role they play in meeting their children's physical needs. He suggests that God's provisions for His children in the Genesis account of creation set the stage for parents to follow suit. Parents also understand the necessity of using discipline to better their children's behavior. The Bible's account of man's fall into sin explains the need for parents to serve in this role. But Dr. Jones submits that stopping here in the biblical story can subconsciously create shortsighted parenting goals of merely helping our children be happy and successful.

There is more to the biblical salvation story, he asserts. Understanding both redemption and consummation (our ultimate destination of heaven) opens our eyes to the fact that parents are called to something more. They are also called to be disciple-makers of their very own children. "Fathers, . . . bring them up in the discipline and instruction of the Lord" (Ephesians 6:4). If we see our children through the eyes of the entire redemption story, we will desire to teach them God's words and ways.

One thing that irritates me is when we only use the Law to try to change our conduct. "You should pray more, give more, serve more, rejoice more." I already know that! I can even add additional behaviors to the to-do list—I should also eat healthier, floss more, sit less, and deal with the piles of paper on my desk. My simply being told the obvious has no effect on my desire or ability to comply. In fact, it highlights the scope of my helplessness.

This applies to parents teaching the faith to their children as well. They know what they're supposed to do. Actually doing it is another matter. The big question is, how can we instill the "want to" rather than the "have to"?

I love the simple phrase found in Romans 2:4: "God's kindness is meant to lead you to repentance." The Gospel holds the promise for change, not the Law. The "shoulds" are helpful in the sense that they show us where we have fallen short, but stopping with them neglects the potential to actually tackle these failures. God lovingly invites us to confess our shortcomings to Him, trusting His "Never Stopping, Never Giving Up, Unbreaking, Always and Forever Love."[9] And to take it one step further, He even goes so far as to provide us His strength to move in another direction.

How does this affect our message to parents? Let's take the issue of family devotions, for example. Rather than "You should have devotions with your children," how about "You have the opportunity to affect your child's faith for a lifetime." Or "How would it feel to have your family life in order so

---

9   Sally Lloyd-Jones, *The Jesus Storybook Bible* (Grand Rapids: Zondervan, 2007).

that the most important issues actually get accomplished?" Or "How would your children describe your family's identity?" Or what if the parents in your church heard someone tell them, "When I was growing up, there was no place I would rather be than with my family during our weekly family night. We played games, had a special meal, and talked about God in our lives."

Statements or questions such as these get to the "why" and provide intrinsic motivation. When the desire to engage children spiritually comes from within rather than from outside forces, the motivation is greater.

STEP 2—CLARIFY THE "HOW"

Start at the beginning.

Change takes place in small increments at a time. Through the years, the first time I met each of my exercise trainers, they would evaluate my physical abilities (or inabilities!) so they would know an appropriate place to begin. Over time, the challenges increase. Likewise, a family who has never prayed together before a meal cannot be expected to extemporaneously pray three times a day. Rather, if they read a short prayer together that has been given them, they have made great strides.

Model activities.

Visualizing an activity is the first step to trying it yourself. Before my trainer asks me to do a new exercise, he demonstrates it himself. Then he corrects my form if I forget and do it improperly.

"Fostering Faith for Preschoolers" was the long moniker for an event in which we tried to do just that. We set up stations in a large room that were staffed by people who would demonstrate activities such as praying before a snack, reading a devotion before bedtime, celebrating a Baptism birthday, and talking about God while taking a walk. After a few minutes at each station, parents were given time to practice the activity with their own children. Our hope was for them to continue these behaviors in their own homes.

Be specific.

Don't expect that everyone understands church lingo. For example, if you want to encourage God talk at home, be specific. Suggest that parents could take a walk with their child and thank God for His beautiful work of creation when they spot a tree in full bloom or a worm wriggling in the dirt. While creating snow angels in the snow, they can point to God's protecting angels. Suggest they look for architectural features that remind them of crosses while riding in the car. Remind them that they can ask God to heal their child's scrape when they put on a bandage. Ask them to tell their children about a time God answered a prayer of their own.

Give tools.

Resources abound in books, and many free samples of home devotions can be found online. You will discover examples that vary in length, some that focus on different ages of children, and others designed to take place each day or once a week. Some devotions simply focus on Bible reading and discussion, while others include additional activities such as singing and games. Some are designed for bedtime, mealtime, or weekly family nights. Give your families several options so they can experiment and see what works best for their home rhythms, personalities, or experience. *Family Time*, *Family Faith Walks*, and even *On-the-Go Prayers* provide a spectrum of devotional opportunities for the family.

Consider the role of milestones/stepping stones.

These programs, briefly described in the previous chapter, provide rhythm and structure to a church's desire to include and guide parents in the spiritual training of their children. Take time to study them in order to discern their differences and how they could support your vision. Some churches use these programs as a place to begin this transitional journey toward nurturing faith at home. Others use them to supplement the parental support they already have in place through other means.

Offer continued support.

This is not a once-and-we're-done effort. Experience tells us how easy it is to slip back into old patterns of behavior. Reversing trends requires patience with ourselves and consistency over time. Be aware that promoting a mind-set change in individuals as well as in the congregation at large will require years, not months.

Mark Holman[10] stresses that the goal of equipping parents to disciple their own children never goes away and entails a long-term commitment. If this goal is integrated into the strategy of the entire church, all the ministries can get on board, support the cause together, and intensify the impact of the message. Ministry silos are seldom effective.

Churches who desire to partner with other nearby congregations to pursue this goal could explore the Family Friendly Partners Network, created by Professor Ben Freudenburg (www.familyfriendlypn.com). Its stated vision and mission is "to train and equip churches to partner with homes to strengthen and pass on faith in Jesus Christ to this generation and those that follow." This network trains clusters of congregations during a three-year process to become intentional Christian family-forming centers that enable parents to deliberately pass on faith in Jesus Christ to the next generation. Clusters currently occur in eight states, and opportunities exist to grow the network.

Reorient current programs.

A new emphasis on championing parents as primary disciple-makers does not mean that current activities and programs must be eliminated. Age-organized programs can and do play an effective role in growing the faith of kids. But existing experiences can be reoriented by using Dr. Jones's TIE test. *TIE* stands for Train, Involve, and Equip parents. He suggests carefully looking at everything that currently takes place and considering how it can be altered to meet those three criteria. He recommends "coordinating every aspect of your present ministry so that parents are acknowledged, equipped, and held accountable as primary disciple-makers in their children's lives."[11]

Despite the fact that parents are primary, there is a place for churches to provide programs and events that support parents' efforts or that reach out to those who have not yet grasped the vision. So let's shift gears and take a closer look at these programs themselves and who makes them possible—those steadfast foot soldiers we call volunteers.

---

10 Mark Holman, *Take It Home* (Ventura: Gospel Light, 2008).
11 T. P. Jones, *Family Ministry Field Guide* (Indianapolis: Wesleyan Publishing House, 2011), 132.

✳ ✳ ✳ ✳

We have created milestone events for parents and children to attend together. First at Baptism and then every other year, on a Sunday morning they come to a special class where they learn how to practice faith in the home. The classes are on family devotions, Scripture memory, prayer, studying the Bible, God talk, and serving. Each class is interactive, and families are sent home with a milestone gift, like an age-appropriate Bible or Scripture memory cards. The following Sunday, our pastor calls the families to the altar for prayer and a blessing.

Sarah Arndt
Children's Ministry Director
Faith Lutheran Church
Troy, MI

✳ ✳ ✳ ✳

I've used faith stepping stones in the past, and this works great because it focuses on a specific age group for a short period of time (2–3 weeks) and equips the parents. I like to use centers with this so parents can practice with their child doing devotions, prayers, simple projects, etc., and ask questions before taking it home and going solo. I also have enjoyed the FAITH5: Holding Your Family Together material from Faith Inkubators. It's a good starting point for parents.

Julie Burgess
Director of Family Life
St. Paul Lutheran Church and School
Ann Arbor, MI

✳ ✳ ✳ ✳

As a preschool director and as a parent, I love the *Jesus Storybook Bible.* It is a beautifully written book that shows Jesus in both the New and Old Testament Bible stories.

Kerri Elliott
FaithKids Preschool Director
Faith Lutheran Church
Troy, MI

✳ ✳ ✳ ✳

The Story Bible is one of the best Bible story books I've seen. This hefty edition provides "130 Stories of God's Love" to help children come to know, as stated in the opening pages, "the love of Jesus, our Savior. The Bible is all about Jesus and you. This Story Bible will show you how and why this is true." On each slick page, beautifully detailed illustrations draw children into the text with the colorful, realistic art drawn large enough for someone to hold the book for everyone to see, point to the pictures illustrating the story being read. . . . *The Story Bible* from Concordia makes an excellent option for any reader, but especially families, small churches, and children's Bible classes where teaching supplies and Bible teachers are likely to be limited. This lovely edition has it all!

Mary Harwell Sayler
Christian poet, writer, and Bible reviewer
http://biblereviewer.blogspot.com
Lake Como, FL

✳ ✳ ✳ ✳

- For parents, we use the FAITH5 format for devotions, and print our own materials in-house.

- We developed a four-year-old "Learning to Pray" milestone and print that in-house.

- We recommend *Prayers on the Go* and also *Blessings and Prayers for Parents*, both by CPH.

- We have given away Advent wreaths with devotions for families to use and share with neighbors.

- We point parents to the Plugged In website for movie reviews.

- Our staff has gone through *Family Friendly Church* by Ben Freuden-berg.

Pastor Bill Wangelin
Our Savior Lutheran Church
Lansing, MI

✳ ✳ ✳ ✳

Each year on Reformation, we give the three-year-olds and second graders Bibles during our church service, and it is a special event. During the time preceding, I teach a class or sometimes several class-es about the importance of family devotions. I try to remind parents to look for teachable moments in their everyday lives.

Janette Haak
Sheepfold Coordinator
St. Luke
Ann Arbor, MI

✳ ✳ ✳ ✳

Discussion Guide for Transitioning toward Growing Faith at Home

Read chapter 4. Gather with your team and discuss the following questions.

1. How can we encourage our parents to grow in their own faith?

2. What life factors limit the time of parents in our church and community?

3. How do you assess the effectiveness of your parents nurturing faith in their homes?

4. What information could stimulate an intrinsic desire for your parents to serve as their children's primary faith-nurturers?

5. Contrast this with examples of legalistic motivation that would have no lasting effect.

6. Identify and prioritize the basic actions you would like parents to specifically do at home with their children. Lead devotions? Pray? Informally talk about God? Enjoy a regular family night? Eat meals together? Play together?

7. What means could you use to encourage these actions?

8. How can you model these desired actions to parents?

9. Will the concept of milestones/stepping stones fit into your overall ministry plan?

10. What tools can you give parents to help them in their spiritual tasks?

11. How will you make a long-term commitment toward carrying forth this vision for parents?

12. How can you reorient your current programs to include parental involvement?

10 Prayers for Your Home

1. Pray that God remains number one in your life.

2. Pray that a desire to be Christlike grows in each member of your family.

3. Pray that you remain committed to gathering your family around God's Word.

4. Pray that a spirit of love and forgiveness permeates your home.

5. Pray for opportunities to have fun with your children.

6. Pray for warmth around your family dinner table.

7. Pray for ways to bring God into your everyday conversations at home.

8. Pray for a commitment to pray with and about your children.

9. Pray that you and your spouse find ways to enjoy each other's company.

10. Pray for committed Christian mentors to build a friendship with your children.

10 Tips for Family Devotions

1. It's never too late to start.

2. Keep it short and simple.

3. Find a regular time that works for you and your family.

4. Do something that fits your family's personality—don't compare with someone else.

5. Experiment—if a plan doesn't work, try something different.

6. Use resources that target the oldest child in your family.

7. Find ways to make your time together enjoyable.

8. Throw perfection out the window.

9. Allow kids to be wiggly.

10. When you fall off the wagon, start again.

What Are the Needs
of Volunteers?

"Through love serve one another." Galatians 5:13

My DCE certification came by way of colloquy from Concordia University, Nebraska, in Seward. Dr. Lisa Keene, who was directing the program at the time, asked a question during her visit to our church: "To what do you attribute the success of your ministry?" Other than God's grace, my answer was the volunteers! It's true—nothing would get done without a team of people committed to sharing Jesus with kids. Because children's ministry often requires more volunteers than other ministries in the church, there always seems to be a shortage.

There was only one time in my life when I recall having an abundance of volunteers. A remarkable young woman who was hoping to get involved in children's ministry was introduced to me. Miraculously, all our classes were fully staffed, so I asked her to observe various ages of children to become more acquainted with our program until a need was discovered. We found her a place to serve, and amazingly enough, she went on to become our summer intern, developed into my administrative assistant, and eventually replaced me as the director of children's ministry. When we thought we were all set, God had a wonderful surprise in store!

Before jumping into the process of enlisting volunteers, two questions are in order. First, is your program one that people want to be part of? Most people want to make a difference in the lives of others. But time is limited, so hours must be used in meaningful ways. If people can make a significant contribution and have fun at the same time, you've created a magical combination. Crafting first-rate and impactful programs precedes the actual recruitment process. Conveying your vision must come before asking volunteers to serve in ministry events.

Second, are you prepared to provide your volunteers with everything they need? This support list includes ample team members, job descriptions, materials, supplies, safety information, encouragement, and training. It is your responsibility to give them every tangible and intangible resource they need to succeed. People need to know exactly what you're asking them to do and what provisions will be given before they can make a commitment.

ENLIST

I used to utilize the word *recruit* and I still do, but I've grown to prefer the term *enlist*. No, we're not trying to get people signed up for the armed forces, but rather we are inviting them to join a mission for God. It's also important to add that the task at hand is more than trying to fill open slots with warm bodies.

I like to think in terms of being a team builder rather than merely a recruiter or even an enlister. Most people find that serving with a team of folks is much more rewarding than working in isolation. The responsibility of building teams does not need to rest on your shoulders alone however. Those already serving may wish to invite their friends to partner with them. The thought of working with friends already makes the task more fun.

Or perhaps the concept of being a talent treasure hunter resonates with you instead. Finding people to serve involves digging deep and getting to know the hidden gems within men, women, and teens—their passions, gifts, skills, interests, and spiritual gifts. People who serve in the areas of their giftedness shine with joy.

When people are asked to do something, they need to know exactly what that role entails and how much time it will require. A job description covers that need very nicely. If job descriptions have not yet been developed, here's a suggestion. Step into the slot you're trying to fill and systematically write down everything you do from start to finish. That is the job description you can confidently give your prospective volunteer. It's important to be up front about all the responsibilities; never sugarcoat what you are asking.

"Do you have any pointers for asking someone to help out?" you may ask. Actually, I do. I have learned that many people either are not aware of their own areas of giftedness or rarely hear others acknowledge and encourage them. This is what an ask might look like. "John, I love seeing you interact with the friends of your kids. We need more kid-loving dads to lead a small group of boys your son's age on Sunday mornings. Have you ever considered getting involved in Sunday School?" Or "Mary, you must love being in the kitchen—the dessert you brought to the ladies' luncheon was a work of art. We're looking for someone to take charge of the creative snacks we hope to serve five mornings in VBS. Might that interest you?" Your invitation to help comes after you point out the trait that you value and is needed.

Don't pressure people to make an on-the-spot decision. Instead, invite them to take some time to think and pray about your request. Ask if you can contact them in a week to discuss their thoughts and to answer any questions they may have. Don't wait for them to respond back to you; chances are good that you won't hear back. Using the examples from the previous paragraph, this is how the conversation could continue. "John, I know I'm catching you off guard. I'd love for you to think and pray about this. Would it be okay if I look you up next Sunday to hear your thoughts?" Or "Mary, I'm certainly not looking for an answer right away. How about thinking and praying about it? I could call you next week to answer any questions you might have. Would that be okay?"

When you call the individual back the following week, be gracious regardless whether they are able to help at that time. If not, thank them for considering and ask them to pray for God's blessing on the ministry. If they do express interest in helping, be sure to tell them about the application process. We don't want to surprise anyone about their need to submit to background checks. We will talk more about this in the next chapter. Be clear and straightforward about all the details involved.

Jim Collins stresses the importance of getting the right people on the bus.[12] Be particular! Do not resort to allowing just anyone to serve with kids; they deserve your best effort. It may be better to use subs or even to cancel a class than to allow someone to serve about whom you have misgivings.

A number of years ago, I learned a difficult lesson. Out of desperation, I took a shortcut and did not call the references on a man who submitted an application to teach. Oh my! Several weeks later, we had a parent open house, and to my embarrassment, this individual was very inappropriately dressed. Afterward, I scurried to call those references and was given information that led me to ask him to discontinue. It was a very sobering and humbling lesson, and I always took references seriously after that incident.

If you have an ongoing shortage of volunteers, may I offer a few recruitment suggestions? These are not quick fixes, but they may help lay a foundation for the long haul.

» Ask the church secretary to give you a list of members or regular attenders who are not currently volunteering. Call them and invite them to serve. A 10-percent affirmative response may not sound like much return for your time investment, but you would be further ahead than when you started!

» Ask the secretary to give you a list of "grandma types" whom you could ask to rock babies in the nursery. Maybe they miss their grandchildren and would be glad to help.

» Invite parents whose children have a hard time separating to be regular helpers. Start small and ask for short increments of time.

» Speak to new-member classes or any other church groups you can think of. Tell them the exciting things about your ministry and how they could form friendships and affect the faith lives of children at the same time.

» Enlist help for one-time events. After the event, ask volunteers who exhibited the traits you desire to help again. Tell them what you admired about their work.

---

12 Jim Collins, *Good to Great* (New York: HarperCollins, 2001).

» Keep updating your list of potential staff. For example, if a young mom mentions that she would be in a better position to help when her three-year-old goes to kindergarten, jot that down and call her in two years.

» Hold a parent open house to acquaint parents with your program. Invite those who seemed to enjoy themselves to occasionally sub. Some people are reluctant to help because they fear not knowing what to do.

» Challenge each person serving to find another individual to tutor in the same thing he or she is currently doing. Replication is great on-the-job training.

» Host a tour on a Sunday morning for anyone interested in hearing more about children's ministry. Be prepared to tell the guests about all the possibilities that exist for service, not just teaching roles.

» Create an annual spring enlistment campaign for summer and fall Sunday School and VBS. Choose a theme, and give creative appeals in the worship service. Prepare handouts or bulletin inserts. Be sure to follow up on all leads. There's nothing that discourages volunteerism more than never returning calls to prospects.

» Work with other ministries to host a fall or January ministry fair. Set up a display to publicize children's ministry, and pass out handouts and free giveaways.

Enlisting is a year-round task. Never let up, even if you are fully staffed. Ample staff must be in place so you can be prepared to welcome any new children God brings into your midst.

EQUIP

Every single person, including you and me, has areas that need growth. As a result, equipping volunteers is never a one-time event. I like to think of training in three stages: Orientation, Individual Support of the Newbies, and Ongoing Development of All Team Members. Let's look at them one at a time.

Level 1: Orientation

Volunteers need to be well informed about what you are asking them to do. An orientation session that lays the foundation for people new to your ministry can be held with an individual or a group. Orientations are also a great way to kick off the school year in the fall for all your volunteers, to prepare for a specific program such as VBS, to become acquainted with you or someone else as a new leader, or to implement new policies or procedures.

Regardless of how many people attend, put yourself in the place of those new folks and imagine what information you would need to do your job effectively. For example, if I were a new classroom helper, I would appreciate a booklet containing the meeting's verbal instructions that I could review at a later date, a calendar, contact information for leaders or peers with whom I will serve, and a job description. If I were teaching, I would also need a class schedule and roster, curriculum, and substitute information. Plan your orientation meeting to meet the needs of the invitees. Is there a need for childcare? What time would be most convenient for them? Will folks come hungry or thirsty? Will they know one another? Prepare accordingly as a way to honor your volunteers.

Orientation also provides an opportunity to teach a new skill. For example, if you have someone who is going to lead music for the first time, don't assume that he or she knows how to do it. Demonstrate how to connect the song to the lesson theme for the day or how to begin teaching a new song by starting with the words to the chorus. Teaching a skill includes demonstration, a practice period, and an opportunity for the learners to present their newfound abilities. This time of learning will ease them into their debut with more confidence and with a clearer understanding of your expectations.

Orientation may also take place in the form of apprenticeship, similar to student teaching. The trainee can initially observe and then move on to lead a few activities and receive feedback from a seasoned leader. He or she can eventually lead a full lesson and receive more input, then finally graduate to leading class solo.

Level 2: Individual Support of the Newbies

Once your new volunteers have begun serving, new questions will most likely arise. We usually don't know what we don't know until we find ourselves in a new position. Only then do we really know what questions to ask. What kind of support might your inexperienced staff need to stay the course? Do everything you can to help these newbies find fulfillment in their roles. It's important to invest time in these relationships. This investment enables you to offer suggestions and to correct situations early, thus avoiding future frustration for them or for you. Giving your new staff a Sunday off to observe another master teacher could be well worth the time it took you to find them a sub. If several volunteers struggle in similar ways, you may want to set a time to discuss a particular issue or strengthen a skill. For example, when our leadership team consistently saw teachers cut corners on our stated bathroom policies, we arranged a half hour to review the rules and practice role-playing. Be creative in helping your volunteers succeed.

Level 3: Ongoing Development of All Team Members

If any of us think we know everything there is to know, it's time to call it a day and hang up our hats. Learning continues throughout our lives. As you receive feedback from your team, you will identify the needs to address. The topics discussed will be in greater depth than those in your original orientation—you need to maintain the interest of those with much experience. Maybe there is a need to keep kids' attention during the lesson or learn how to build relationships with the kids. Perhaps it's how to teach kids to pray aloud, how to teach from a Gospel perspective, or how to deal with special needs. You could share teaching information yourself or invite speakers to come to your church to present on an area of their expertise. The challenge is how to make the learning fun and encourage participation. Training may be as brief as a breakfast meeting before Sunday School or a luncheon afterward when everyone is already at church. Offering childcare would help those parents who may be unable to attend otherwise. Ongoing development may include all volunteers or may target specialized groups. You will want to use every training opportunity to include a time of prayer and to reiterate the V/P/M (vision, purpose, and mission) of your ministry. Ask the pastor to come and personally express his appreciation—that gesture means so much to children's staff who can easily feel taken for granted.

Take key leaders to seminars, workshops, or conferences as a means to enhance learning and to grow community and enthusiasm. Utilize books, articles, magazines, websites, podcasts, YouTube videos, CDs, DVDs—anything you can think of to equip those who work with you and to help their joy quota grow.

APPRECIATE

We do not serve in order to be appreciated, but when appreciation is absent, discouragement can easily set in. Paul exhorts us to encourage one another, and the challenging task of working with children provides the perfect opportunity to do so. After a weekend of babysitting my young grandsons, I told them, "I love being with you." In return, I heard, "I love being with you too, Grandma." Those loving and encouraging words from children immediately removed any weariness and still play over and over in my mind.

Appreciation need not be in the form of material gifts, although there is nothing wrong with tangible gestures of gratitude. Gifts may be as simple as an Almond Joy candy bar with the words "Watching you share Jesus' love gives me Joy." Sharing words of affirmation, offering a cup of coffee, sending a birthday card, acknowledging volunteers in a worship service, writing a note—all are simple ways of showing love and care and appreciation to those who provide the backbone of our ministry.

EVALUATE

At first glance, this word sparks fear in the hearts of some leaders. We tend to think, "Who am I to tell another person how they're doing?" or "Who wants to hear that they are doing a crummy job?" But neither reaction accurately reflects the core purpose of evaluation.

In reality, aren't you already constantly assessing situations? As you walk down the hall and see a dirty stain on the carpet, you make a mental note to do something about it. When you notice a teacher telling children "Jesus loves you" as they leave, you warm at the thought of that send-off and remind yourself to commend the teacher. If you detect that fewer and fewer children attend your Christmas program each year, you will want to explore the reasons and brainstorm other possibilities. Evaluation alerts you to those things you want to keep doing, those things you want to start doing, and those things you want to stop doing.

Each spring, I like to take a few moments one at a time with volunteers and ask about their experiences. What went well? What needs improvement? What advice could they offer me? Where did they receive their greatest satisfaction? If something new was introduced during their tenure, what was their impression about the change? Would they want to continue serving in their current role? Receiving this input from those in the trenches is invaluable in preparing for the future. It also validates staff by showing respect for their opinions.

REDIRECT

Individuals who serve in positions that suit their giftedness do so with joy and energy. Square pegs in round holes chafe and experience self-doubt and frustration until they are ready to quit. When we observe this dissonance, we must step in and intervene for the well-being of our volunteers, the children, and ourselves.

I remember a small-group leader who repeatedly expressed frustration to me over the behavior of his group of boys. After talking with him about his life interests, we discerned that he would much prefer to work in the tech booth than in his current role. When this change was made, he patiently mentored many young people as they learned the tech skills he taught them. Many of these students graduated from serving in children's ministry and now partner with the adults in the tech ministry in "big church."

If there is not a good ministry fit for volunteers, consider these possible steps:

» Offer more training.

» Invite them to work with a different age group of children.

» Connect them with another team or individual.

» Give them time to partner with a mentor.

» Suggest another area of service that requires different gifts or time availability.

» Offer a break from service if they need time to deal with a personal issue.

Don't overlook the possibility that the problem may not rest with the volunteers. Rather, it may point to a need to modify an issue in your ministry approach or culture. Perhaps an individual got blindsided by expectations that weren't clear up front. Maybe a helper was caught off guard while learning later on about the requirement to attend monthly meetings. Perhaps the supervisor didn't provide enough initial training. Maybe the volunteer felt pushed into accepting a position because of the need, regardless of the fit. We must accept ownership for these bloopers and make the needed corrections.

But what if an individual is serving poorly and is not upholding the values that define your ministry? Speaking with someone in this type of thorny circumstance is never an easy task and is admittedly risky. The conversation may turn out badly. Prayerful preparation is the key. Love for the individual, not irritation, must be your motivation. Almost every time I have had to speak with someone about an issue, I learned that person had also experienced frustration and recognized the need for change. Only God could have paved the way for these potentially difficult conversations. If anticipating a particular discussion is daunting, you may want to seek another person's counsel to offer you a different perspective.

I recall a difficult time when a team member was displaying passive aggressive behavior that was quite disruptive to the rest of the group. I expressed my frustration to a counselor friend with the words, "I have bent over backwards with this person!" He thought for a moment and finally asked, "What will it take for you to stand up straight?" I immediately knew that I had to address the situation. The behavior was inappropriate and was affecting others. There was a period of hurt feelings, but this individual found meaningful service elsewhere and the team realized a level of health that had not been experienced in some time.

While driving to a conference some years ago with my pastor, I asked him, "Can you ever fire a volunteer?" His affirmative answer gave me the courage to follow through with that difficult task on several occasions. The last resort in this redirection process is dismissal. There are deal breakers when a volunteer cannot be permitted to continue in his or her role.

» Physical, sexual, or emotional abuse

» Rejection of faith

» Not compliant with stated leader requirements regarding lifestyle, habits, or theology

» Destructive attitude

» Refusal to comply with leadership

» Unable to cope at this stage of life

Those who work with children have a high calling—we represent Jesus. We humbly remain on our knees confessing our own shortcomings as we beg for the Spirit's strength to invite others to serve God and His people.

* * * *

I am so blessed with volunteers who have been teaching for many years. However, this year I also needed quite a few just weeks before we were to begin. I asked a few key people, but did not BEG! I will NOT put a person in a classroom just to be a warm body; it is not good for anyone involved. I want teachers and volunteers to be there because they enjoy it and look forward to it. I pray and ask God to bring the people to mind for me to contact and let Him do the work. This year was not any different, but I am so thankful for the volunteers we have, especially the teachers who say, "One hour is just not enough time!"

Janette Haak
Sheepfold Coordinator
St. Luke
Ann Arbor, MI

* * * *

Inventory for Serving Volunteers

After reading chapter 5, take an inventory of how your own church serves volunteers. What next steps can you take in each of the following areas?

Laying a foundation: Ministry improvements needed before asking people to serve . . .

_____

_____

_____

Enlisting: Names of potential teammates or people with specialized gifts . . .

_____

_____

_____

Ways we will try to fill some of our staffing needs . . .

_____

_____

_____

Equipping: Our staff needs coaching in the areas of Orientation, Individual Support, or Ongoing Development . . .

_____

_____

_____

Appreciating: We can express appreciation in the following ways . . .

Evaluating: Steps we can take to evaluate staff skills and satisfaction . . .

Redirecting: A conversation is needed with this individual who is not experiencing a good ministry fit . . .

Volunteers Need to Apply?

"Whoever causes one of these little ones who believe in me to sin, it would be better for him to have a great millstone fastened around his neck and to be drowned in the depth of the sea."
Matthew 18:6

Safety is the number-one issue that concerns parents today. Moms and dads who don't feel that their children would be safe in your care simply will not bring them to your church events. Getting policies in place to ensure that your programs and the personnel leading them provide a safe haven will admittedly take effort on your part. But this work of prevention is much more pleasant than the labor required to resolve some incident of impropriety or negligence. A prayer for protection of our children is frequently in my heart when they are in our care.

Many hours will be spent with your leadership team as you format policies and procedures to fit your church's individual needs. Leaders from other churches or your district office can share materials to help ease you into the process. Months from now when you gladly reach the finish line, the church council or other regulating body can place their stamp of approval on your work to free you to confidently put the new guidelines into practice.

If you are a volunteer leader at your church, it would be very understandable if you experience some hesitation as we proceed. You may even be asking yourself, "What authority do I have to ask my friends for applications and carry out background checks on them? I'm only a volunteer myself!" Discuss any hesitancy with your pastor, the board of education, or the church council.

Someone does need to take the initiative to screen volunteers. Perhaps a secretary or other staff person could handle this security task for the entire church. But don't hesitate to consider that God may have chosen you to see this through. I love reading Moses' reaction to God's call in the Book of Exodus because I've responded in like manner on more than one occasion. "Who am I? . . . I don't talk well. . . . Who should I say sent me? . . . What if they don't listen?" God's response is equally poignant: "I will be with you. I will provide for your needs." He did provide then, and He continues to do so.

The placement procedure for volunteers will include these four main components:

» A policy manual

» A face-to-face interview

» The application

» References and background checks

Ideally, prospective volunteers should be told that before they are placed with children, they will be asked to undergo this entire application and screening process. Your church may have all or none of these components in place at the moment. If you are creating placement procedures for the first time, tackle the project one step at a time. The place to begin is with the policy manual.

THE POLICY MANUAL

Policy manuals are an expected norm these days. Having policies and procedures in writing helps volunteers avoid surprises because the document clarifies expectations right at the beginning. A manual also demonstrates to your church's insurance company that your church is complying with its terms. The insurance company at my previous church would even call periodically to question our application and screening process, making sure we did not present a risk to them. Therefore, a good place for you to begin is with your church's insurance company itself. It may offer you a policy manual template that can be edited for your church's distinct needs.

As you brainstorm with your team about what your volunteers need to know, review any draft from your insurance company, and examine samples from other churches, you will note similarities in the following categories:

» Welcome letter from the director

» Mission/vision/purpose/values

» Statement of faith

» Leader requirements

» Safety policies (more details will follow in chapter 7)

—Two-worker rule

—Drop-off and pick-up procedures

—Physical touch

—Bathroom procedures

—Injuries

—Emergencies

—Discipline

—Peanut policy

—Child abuse

Plan to continually edit the manual you create; it is always a work in progress. For example, after one of our teen leaders became known for his marijuana use, we realized that our manual made no mention of drugs and quickly made that correction. When cell phone usage became more prominent, we added the request that volunteers not use phones while working with the children. Privacy concerns pushed us to prevent volunteers from posting photos of their classes on Facebook. And in today's world of social media, wisdom would lead us to create additional guidelines in this area.

New volunteers will welcome this information in writing. As you tell existing volunteers about the need to reassure parents about the safety of their children, they will understand that protecting children is one tangible way to show them our love and care.

FACE-TO-FACE INTERVIEW

If you already know your prospective volunteer, this step can be as simple as an informal conversation to explore an area of service, answer questions, or share information. If you don't know the individual well, here is your opportunity to begin an ongoing relationship. While working at my larger congregation, people whom I had never met before would frequently volunteer their service, especially at the start of each season in the sports program. A conversation would take place formally in my office or informally over a cup of coffee in the lobby. Meeting someone in person provides so much more tangible and intangible information about an individual than an unseen conversation over the phone.

Why is an interview so critical? Ultimately, we want to help our volunteers experience a good ministry fit—to love what they do and to love the people with whom they serve. Getting to know them helps us work together toward a good match. As we learn more about their interests, we may need to guide them to another service area that was not originally considered but could be better suited. The time spent together opens up the door to listen and offer care and support should hardships become known. This step also conveys to the applicant that serving children is an important responsibility. It sends the message that we are serious about who works with our precious children; don't bother to apply if you have something to hide!

One of the categories to include in a policy manual is a list of leader requirements. During your interview, it provides guidelines for the characteristics you are seeking in a prospective volunteer. These requirements will benefit you immensely as you discern whether the interviewee is ready to be placed in a teaching or leadership position with children.

On occasion, after learning that a prospective volunteer was living with a girlfriend or boyfriend, I would explain that our policy would not allow us at the moment to place him or her with children because the lives of our staff need to uphold scriptural standards to the best of our abilities. It's better to have this challenging conversation at the beginning of the application process than to catch someone off guard after he or she has been placed. But if you do face any personnel issues later on, the leader requirements provide a reference point for discussion. Consider the following for your list of requirements:

» Is a baptized believer who regularly participates in worship and the Lord's Supper

» Engages in Bible study and prayer

» Agrees with our church's statement of faith

» Has regularly worshiped at our church for at least six months

» Loves kids

» Lives a life of sexual purity

» Does not use illegal drugs

» Is at a place emotionally, physically, and spiritually where able to serve

» Meets with the director

» Completes the application process

» Agrees to abide by the policies in the manual

» Receives positive references

» Attends training

THE APPLICATION

An application form confirms the prospective volunteer's desire to serve in ministry with children. It provides written information and gives permission for you to complete the entire application process. It ultimately deters folks you would not want to serve as role models for children. Other details requested on an application may include the following:

» Contact information

» Date of birth

» Occupation

» Family members

» Previous experience with children

» Church background

» Hobbies, interests

» Current ministry desires

» How faith life is maintained

» References (no relatives)

» Permission to do a background check

» Expresses willingness to abide by policies in manual

» States agreement with leader requirements and statement of faith

» Copy of driver's license

Whether completing the written application or holding the one-on-one interview comes first is immaterial. The information requested on this document can provide a basis for your conversation, or the document can simply formalize the previous conversation you had and grant permission to complete the application process.

Some of the written responses you receive may require a follow-up conversation. I recall a teaching moment when, in response to the manual's statement of faith, a woman admitted that she didn't believe in creation. On another occasion, in response to the leader requirements, an individual expressed her struggle with mental health issues. She graciously agreed to postpone working with children and help prepare crafts in the meantime while she and her doctor worked toward regaining health. People who risk telling you about their personal challenges or diverse viewpoints need to be commended for their honesty and courage.

A number of years ago, our outreach pastor challenged me to consider allowing non-Christians or parents not attending church to assist in our children's programs. I did not want to let go of our high standards of Christ-followers serving as role models to the children. Yet I also knew that some of these committed, loving parents who wanted to offer their time or expertise to our ministries would offer a valuable service. The compromise at which we arrived served both purposes. We created another application form, which also required all the same safety protocols. But rather than asking questions about their faith life, we substituted another question: "Do you agree not to teach anything contrary to the beliefs listed in the policy manual?" We also placed the individual with another strong Christian leader who knew his or her role also included spiritually mentoring the new applicant.

Because of the personal nature of these documents, store them in a locked file or a secure place along with the accompanying background checks and references. You will also need to keep a confidential file for people who may *not* be qualified to serve after you have completed the entire application process.

REFERENCES AND BACKGROUND CHECKS

After receiving and reviewing the application, you will need to follow up on the references provided and the appropriate background checks. Know that neither of these is foolproof; they reduce risks but cannot completely eliminate them. Preschool and day-care staffs are required to undergo background checks by law; because volunteers work with children as well, we uphold the same requirements. This measure goes a long way in easing the minds of vigilant parents.

Ask for two references from non-family members, along with their contact information. Some churches also ask for a reference from the previous church attended. You will need to prepare a list of questions to ask the people whose names were submitted. These may include the following:

» Name of the applicant and person giving referral

» How long have you known the individual and in what context (friend, work acquaintance)?

» How do you feel he or she will do in a setting with children? How does he or she relate to children?

» How would you describe his or her temperament?

» Describe this individual's commitment and responsibility (team player, punctual).

» What concerns, if any, would you have with allowing this individual to work with children?

» What additional information should we know regarding this individual that could be helpful?

» Date and name of the person conducting the interview if by phone

This feedback can be gleaned via phone call, mail, or email. The completed questionnaire can be attached to the original application and securely filed away. Remember that if you ask for references, you must follow up on them.

A church can either conduct its own background checks or hire a company to handle the details for them. One of many companies that offer background screening services for both employees and volunteers is Protect My Ministry, an LCMS national contract provider (www.protectmyministry.com). Completing your own screenings is more cost effective (most are free or charge a minimal fee and can be done online) but can be labor intensive. You will want to study both options and discuss them with your pastor, board, or council. Either way, you will need to create a workable system and identify the person responsible for each step in the application process.

Various types of background checks exist, and companies offer different degrees of searches. Know, however, that no one can guarantee 100-percent accuracy. Background checks vary from state to state, and procedural changes are frequently made, so you will need to keep current with each registry if you handle the process yourself. I would suggest that you find an attorney to help you sort through the complicated details. Some searches require a date of birth, driver's license number, or Social Security number, so be sure to ask for these on your application form. Some potential background checks are as follows:

» State Criminal Records Search—searches state police records and reveals arrests and convictions for felonies and misdemeanors

» National Sex Offender Registry Search—provides photos for identification purposes

» National Criminal Records Search—identifies convicted felons and those who have served time in prison for more than one year

» Motor Vehicle Records Search—searches for traffic violations and is required if staff or volunteers drive children or youth

» Miscellaneous Searches—additional searches can be done if needed, such as County Criminal Records Search, Social Security Number Verification, Address History Trace, Credit History Report, etc.

I recommend a minimum of the first two searches listed above for all volunteers.

Incidents of past indiscretion may surface as searches are conducted. I believe the best approach is a direct conversation with the individual concerned. "Sam, when I did your background check, I noted that you were convicted of two DUIs back in the nineties. What can you tell me about that?" (This and theft are the most common infractions, in my experience.) This approach gives the individual the opportunity to admit to foolish mistakes made fifteen years ago, and it enables you to reassure the person that this prior infraction would not prevent him or her from working with children today. Unfortunately, record-keeping errors do exist, and notifying the individual gives him or her the opportunity to correct inaccuracies.

A deal breaker, however, would be a conviction of abuse. Even if a person with a previous record insists that he or she poses no risk to children, that person must not be permitted to have contact with children, regardless of how long ago the incident occurred. Forgiveness does not negate consequences of past behavior. If you are uncertain how to respond to search results, seek guidance from your church attorney.

Finally, consider how often you will update the procedures and repeat the background checks. Parents will be grateful that you have done due diligence in screening those who care for their children.

Traits That Suit Selected Volunteer Positions

People who have been gifted with the following traits could be just what is needed to fill these volunteer roles.

Role	Suitable Traits	Person Who Comes to Mind Who Could Serve
Teacher	Desires to share faith, welcoming, can keep kids' attention, able to communicate clearly, respects kids, can guide assistants, instills the confidence of parents, is aware of the surroundings, able to plan	
Classroom Helper	Enjoys kids, loves to assist another, willing to be guided, cooperative, respects kids	
Greeter	Friendly, warm, desires to help people feel comfortable, creates a positive first impression	
Music Leader	Can keep kids' attention, loves to worship God, can sing, clearly explains new songs, willing to practice	
Small-Group Leader	Able to build relationships with kids, can keep kids engaged, wants to apply God's Word to kids' lives, able to pray aloud about their needs	
Large-Group Presenter	Can keep kids' attention, explains Bible truths in clear and interesting ways, engaging, takes the time to practice	
Superintendent	Self-starter, leader, attentive to detail while aware of the big picture, planner, encourager, willing to make needed changes	
Supply-Room Organizer	Loves to organize and make order from chaos, can choose the time to help	
Craft Preparer	Enjoys crafts and behind-the-scenes service, resourceful, wants to work from home	
Tech Support	Comfortable with technology, can quickly solve problems	

How to Process a New Volunteer for a Position Working with Children

Use this checklist to make sure you cover all the steps in preparing a volunteer to serve.

_____ Conduct a face-to-face interview. If the individual meets all the leader requirements listed in your handbook, continue on. If not, maintain the relationship or find another serving opportunity until he or she is able to successfully complete the application process.

_____ Give the application and policy manual. (May do this before the interview.)

_____ Receive the completed application. Discuss omissions, clarify inaccuracies, and discuss differing viewpoints that have been expressed.

_____ Sign the application.

_____ Follow up on references.

_____ Complete security checks.

_____ Attach the reference referrals and security checks to the application and store in a secure location in the church.

_____ Discuss the job description with the applicant.

_____ Give and review teaching materials if needed.

_____ Introduce the new volunteer to teaching partners.

_____ Show the available resources and classroom location.

_____ Give the new volunteer an official nametag.

_____ Welcome the new volunteer on the first day of serving.

_____ Frequently express your appreciation.

_____ After two months of service, talk with the new volunteer to see if she or he is feeling comfortable. Support the individual as needed.

Sample Applications

FaithKids Volunteer Application
Faith Lutheran Church/Troy
(For Adults Attending Faith)

Date_____

Name_____
       Last   First   Middle   Maiden

Date of Birth_____
                 month/date/year

Address _____ **City** _____ **Zip**_____

Home Phone_____   **Cell Phone** _____

Email _____

Occupation _____ **Marital Status**_____

Children's Names/Ages_____

_____

How long have you attended Faith Lutheran Church?_____

Have you attended Faith's New Member Class (3 Solas)? ☐ Yes   ☐ No

Do you fully understand and agree with the Statement of Faith listed in FaithKids Policy Manual ? ☐ Yes   ☐ No

Comments:_____
_____
_____

Do you agree to abide by the Leader Requirements and other policies and procedures as listed in FaithKids Policy Manual? ☐ Yes   ☐ No

Comments:_____
_____
_____

Is your spouse supportive of the commitment that you want to make to the Children's Ministries? ☐ Yes   ☐ No   ☐ Uncertain   ☐ Not Applicable
_____
_____

2015

Permission granted from Faith Lutheran Church, Troy, MI.

FaithKids Volunteer Application
Faith Lutheran Church/Troy
(Under 18 years of age)

Date_____

Name_____
        Last   First   Middle

Address_____ City & Zip_____

Mother's Name_____

Father's Name_____

Date of Birth_____ Grade in School_____

Home Phone Number _____

Cell Phone _____Email _____

What is the name of your home church?_____
What city is it located in?_____

Why do you consider yourself a Christian?_____
_____
_____
_____

What experiences have you had with children?_____
_____
_____
_____

Do you fully understand and agree with the Statement of Faith listed in FaithKids Training
Manual ? ☐ Yes   ☐ No
_____
_____

(Please complete back side of form also)

2015

What Do My Volunteers Need to Know about Safety?

"We endure anything rather than put an obstacle in the way of the gospel of Christ." 1 Corinthians 9:12

Talking about safety can be wearisome; I want to get to the main point of why we serve children—Jesus! It's easy to get bogged down with burdensome details and stray from our core mission. Talking about safety can also instill fear, a menace that Jesus continually addressed. So why continue pursuing this topic of safety?

In the Scripture reference above, Paul underscores his willingness to put up with anything so the message of the Gospel is not hindered. He goes on to say in verses 19–20, 22–23, "For though I am free from all, I have made myself a servant to all, that I might win more of them. To the Jews I became as a Jew, in order to win Jews. . . . I have become all things to all people, that by all means I might save some. I do it all for the sake of the gospel, that I may share with them in its blessings."

Because the culture in which we live is highly focused on child safety, churches must speak to that value as well if we want parents to entrust their children to our care. Providing a safe place is not the ultimate purpose of our existence, of course, but it is a means to achieve our mission to reach kids for Christ.

When your guidelines are in place and included in your policy manual, you will be amazed at the confidence and freedom you and your volunteers will experience as you interact with the children God has brought your way.

DROP-OFF AND PICK-UP PROCEDURES

Children need to be supervised at all times on your site, either by their parents and guardians or by your church staff. To relay this message, designate a check-in and check-out area in each classroom where parents sign in and sign out their children. Establishing this new procedure may be most challenging in a smaller setting where everyone knows each other and children have been allowed to freely roam the building. But what if God brings new families to your church? Lay the foundation now so if you experience an increase in enrollment, you will be prepared to safely supervise even more children. We want to provide a sense of confidence and security for new parents entering your building with their children and forming their first impressions.

The most effective safety procedure is to offer duplicate nametags upon check-in, one for the child to wear and the other for the parent to present at pick-up. Several options exist depending on your financial resources. You can create duplicate nametags by hand, purchase predesigned tags with sticky backs, or invest in computer software and a printer that records attendance and issues nametags simultaneously.

I recall a challenging family circumstance in which the children's father was not allowed by court order to be alone with his children. Thankfully, these above-mentioned procedures kept us from contributing to a potentially dangerous situation by not allowing him to take his children after class.

If someone different needs to pick up a child and would not have access to the duplicate nametag, the person bringing the child must give written permission before the child is released to the second individual. You may want to consider creating a check-in form that provides a column for the child's name, another for the parent's location or contact information, and a third for the name of someone different retrieving the child. Asking the second individual to provide identification serves as an extra precaution. Don't wait—the time to initiate these new procedures is now!

HEALTH

Physical well-being applies to both the staff and the children participating. No one should be allowed to jeopardize the health of others.

Many churches create a sick-child policy that enables workers to refuse children with fevers, coughs, rashes, red eyes, or green noses. I have met parents desperate for a break who have brought their obviously ill children to the nursery. We certainly understand their need for respite, but it's not fair to expose other children to someone else's sniffles and sneezes. My rule of thumb is this: would I want my own children or grandchildren to play with a child with these symptoms? If not, I ask the parents to take their child with them.

Toys that infants and toddlers put in their mouths must be washed after each session, and swings and infant seats should be sprayed with disinfectant after each use. All toys should be hand-washed or run through the dishwasher at least twice a year. In order to keep little ones, your staff, and the area sanitized, you will want to provide diaper-changing guidelines for the nursery workers. Ideas of cleanliness differ immensely; set the standard for your church.

When children register for a program such as Sunday School or VBS, ask parents to identify food allergies or other important health issues. Most churches and schools no longer serve food containing peanuts in order to accommodate children with life-threatening conditions. To put inquiring parents' minds at ease, consider displaying a list of ingredients for the snacks to be served.

Finally, first-aid supplies need to be within easy reach in each room. Bandages, antiseptic wipes, antibiotic ointment, instant cold compresses, latex gloves, vomit absorber—there's nothing more frustrating than searching all over the building when the need for one of these items is immediate! You may want to consider asking several leaders to take CPR training. If your church has an AED, be sure your staff knows its location, as well as the location of landlines should a 911 call be necessary. Parents must be informed of any accidents or incidents, even the minor ones, and these should be recorded on an incident report form. This document can be as simple as a written description of the injury with the date and signature of the person providing the information. Be sure to save this information in a location where it can be found again should the need arise.

TWO-WORKER RULE

Children must never be alone with an adult or teen volunteer while they are under your care. The two-worker policy ensures this does not happen. This not only provides extra protection for the child, but it also protects staff against false allegations. Some churches even require a third person be present when a married couple serves together.

Going one step further, classroom doors should be kept open (gates can prevent little escapees!) or windows installed so the room can be observed at all times. One-way glass beautifully provides that opportunity without distraction for the children. Our goal is to go out of our way to build parental trust in the care we offer their precious children.

ADULT-TO-CHILD RATIOS

Establishing a ratio for your ministry helps clarify staffing needs and ensures adequate care for the children. Guidelines suggested by childcare licensing can be a place to start, but I much prefer a smaller ratio, such as 1 adult to 2 infants, 1 adult to 4 toddlers, 1 adult to 6 preschoolers, and 1 adult to 8 elementary children. Since even this number of children can be a handful depending on personalities, additional teen assistants would be extremely beneficial.

Unforeseen circumstances always arise. What if more children attend on a given Sunday than expected or a teacher is ill and cannot come? There are several options to consider:

» Prerecruit a last minute sub to call for such emergencies.

» Combine two groups of children so one teacher isn't alone.

» Ask spare staff from another class to pinch hit.

» Ask parents bringing their children to remain.

» Decline accepting children until the staffing is resolved.

None of these ideas may be ideal, but be prepared with a backup plan. You're sure to need it!

BATHROOM POLICY

As mentioned before, children need to be supervised at all times—this includes in the bathroom while under your care. Thus, allowing a child to leave the classroom alone is unacceptable. But at the same time, we also clarified that children are not to be alone in a room with an adult or teen—this also includes in the bathroom. How to handle the quandary? Having plenty of staff is the key.

Ask a volunteer to accompany a child to the bathroom and while the child waits at the door, the worker can check to see if it is occupied. When vacant, the worker can wait by the door while the child uses the restroom and eventually accompany the child back to the room. Older children could be sent in pairs without the company of a volunteer.

Younger children who may need more intimate assistance require two workers to be present, one to personally assist and the other to observe. If a whole class takes a bathroom break at the same time, two volunteers may enter the room together to supervise. As you can tell, upholding security policies require lots of staff.

Speaking of the bathroom, a bathroom accident will happen sooner or later with little ones. Keep extra clothing and plastic bags for wet clothes on hand for when the need arises. Socks, underwear, and sweatpants bought at a garage or rummage sale fit the bill perfectly.

EMERGENCIES

One Sunday morning, the electricity went off in our entire building. Interior rooms without windows such as the nursery suddenly plunged into darkness. Children cried, teachers panicked, and parents rushed out of the worship service to check on their children. That chaotic morning gave us the impetus to stock each room with flashlights, something we had never considered before.

Would your volunteers know where to take their children outdoors should there be a fire? Or where children can safely gather for a tornado warning? What if a child becomes lost? How would you enlist a search party? If the child is present but the parents are "lost," where would you have the child wait?

Thinking through all these scary possibilities can be quite depressing. It certainly places me on my knees begging God to send His angels of protection. Should an emergency arise, knowing exactly what to do helps ease anxiety.

A good place to start when creating guidelines is with your local school system. Because schools are required to think through every possible emergency, the work they have already done can help you craft your own procedures. Be sure to post directions in the classrooms as well as in your manual.

TOUCH

Children need kind and loving gestures! And yet, in this day and age of litigation, some volunteers fear touching children at all. Defining appropriate and inappropriate contact can be helpful. Taking a child's hand to lead him from one activity to another, holding a crying preschooler, putting your arm around a child's shoulder to offer comfort—these are totally appropriate acts of kindness.

Inappropriate touch involves common sense—kissing a child, coaxing a child to kiss you, extended hugging or tickling, touching a child in any area that would be covered by a bathing suit (except when assisting a very young child with toileting in the presence of another person), or carrying older children or having them sit on your lap.

One of my creative college students devised the "no-no square." She demonstrated by touching one shoulder, then the other shoulder, followed by each hip while counting 1, 2, 3, 4. What a creative way to teach children the area of their body that is private!

As an aside, if you have young people helping with the little ones, you may want to require them to be age 16 to carry infants and toddlers.[13]

CHILD ABUSE

We pray we never meet a child suffering from any type of neglect or abuse—physical, sexual, or emotional. But should that situation arise, share your suspicions with your pastor or staff member who will advise you on

---

13 See also Scottie May, *Children Matter* (Grand Rapids: Eerdmans, 2005), 322.

the reporting steps to take. Your allegations will be kept confidential by Social Services. Do not interrogate a child regarding any suspected abuse. This will be conducted by a trained professional should the need arise. And by all means, this information is not to be communicated to additional church members or friends.

Once you have established your own church's safety guidelines, included them in your own volunteer policy manual, and communicated them to your volunteers, the only step that remains is implementing them. Prepare to gently remind volunteers when you observe infractions (and you will!). The children are worth it!

Check-In and Check-Out Form

Child's Name	Person Bringing Child	Location and Contact Information	Different Person Picking Up Child (If Applies)

What Do My Teachers Need to Know about Children?

"You formed my inward parts; You knitted me together in my mother's womb. I praise You, for I am fearfully and wonderfully made." Psalm 139:13–14

I hated speech classes in high school. To increase my self-confidence on speech days, I borrowed clothes from my friend across the street, knowing that her clothes were much "cooler" than my own. So years later when I *wanted* to take an adult education class in speech, even I was surprised!

One of the most important factors, the instructor told us, was to know our audience. A speech would fall on deaf ears if it didn't connect with the people listening. It was important to know the audience's age, gender, culture, interests, beliefs, level of knowledge about the topic, why it was important to them, and what they hoped to learn from you. Speaking to people without knowing their perspective would result in disinterested and disconnected listeners.

This advice applies to teaching children as well. During lesson preparation, our audience must be in the forefront of our minds. We are teaching *children*, not merely topics. Frankly, I have done both. When I started presenting the children's messages on Sunday mornings at our church, a combination of nervousness and not yet knowing the children kept me focused on the material. Now during times of planning, individual faces of children come to mind as I prayerfully wonder what and how God wants me to communicate to them.

Jesus, the Master Teacher, focused beautifully on His audience whether it was a single individual in a unique life situation or a crowd of people, and He tailored His message accordingly. He challenged the rich young ruler to give away his wealth. He presented Himself as the bread of life to His disciples after they witnessed the miracle of the feeding of the five thousand. He sharply confronted the Pharisees with their self-righteous attitudes. Each message perfectly fit His listeners' needs.

We, too, must know our audience. Knowing general traits of children is the place to start, but then we must move on to the specific attributes of those girls and boys whom we serve.

AGE-LEVEL CHARACTERISTICS

A teacher I once knew wanted to talk to the parents of his children about their misbehavior in class. Before resorting to that measure, I visited the room and discovered conduct that was quite appropriate and predictable for the children's developmental age. It was the teacher's expectations that were off base.

Helping instructors understand age-level characteristics can resolve this disparity between reality and unrealistic beliefs. Teachers who grasp these concepts are better able to relate to the children and experience less frustration in the process. Knowing physical, social, behavioral, emotional, and spiritual attributes helps teachers avoid methods that are too simplistic or too sophisticated. Knowing the students they teach is a must for teaching that connects with the heart.

CHILD DEVELOPMENT

The aforementioned age-level characteristics are ultimately based on the work of child development theorists such as Jean Piaget and Erik Erikson. Piaget's greatest contribution for our purposes in his Theory of Cognitive

Development is his reminder that young children are concrete, literal thinkers. Perhaps you've seen the drawing of the Mount of Olives by a child—a mountain made of a pile of green olives! Children's thinking becomes more analytical around age 7, and by age 11, they are able to reason more abstractly. We must challenge teachers to translate abstract spiritual truths into concepts children can bring into their own worlds.

Erik Erikson's Theory of Psychosocial (personality) Development helps further our understanding of children at various stages. He believes that the biggest learning infants undertake is acquiring trust. Trust is developed in a familiar environment through caring and consistent caregivers who feed children when hungry, change them when soiled, and hold them when afraid or wanting contact. What a high calling for nursery staff to take on this role of "being Jesus with skin on"! When church caregivers love those babies, they lay a foundation of trust these children will need in order to know and love God.

As children graduate from the nursery and begin attending classes for toddlers, new skills can be taught that honor their growing sense of independence. Anyone familiar with tots of this age recognizes the "me do it" and "no" phase. Praise and encouragement are important traits for teachers to display when kids want to experiment on their own. Experiencing human examples of unconditional love lays the foundation for children to receive God's absolute, unconditional love for them.

Preschoolers are mastering many more basic life skills and love to question and use their active imaginations. What fun it is to explore with these children, to teach them new things, and to see their joyful learning! As they realize that some activities are difficult and others can result in adult disapproval, an atmosphere of love and forgiveness paves the way for children to experience these same qualities in God.

Finally, as children enter school, social and academic pressures develop, and children begin to compare themselves to others. It is vital to teach that our worth is not tied into our successes in life. Ephesians 2:8–10 is very clear that we do not earn God's approval by what we do; we have already received it simply by who we are. Kids (and adults!) need to know this truth. As children mature, many begin to challenge the simple faith of their childhood. These children need the gift of faith-filled adults who respond calmly and candidly to their searching.

James Fowler is known for taking these theories one step further and applying them to faith development. He believes that children form their image of God around the image they have of their parents. In other words, if their parents are warm, loving, and forgiving, they will see God through that same lens. If parents are overly busy or neglectful, children may see God as uninvolved. If strict and harsh, they may become afraid of God. When children see their parents pray, worship, and make God a priority, these values will become their own. Fowler's thoughts still place me on my parental knees, and my kids are all grown up!

John Westerhoff is a twentieth-century scholar who spoke and wrote extensively on the faith development of children. I heard him speak many years ago at a teachers conference in our district. He uses a tree analogy for faith development that is very compatible with our Lutheran doctrine of Baptism. Faith grows like tree rings that are sequential; each ring that is added changes the tree, but builds on what was previously developed. He warns against filling children's heads with facts without touching hearts with God's love and an experience of Christian community.

Teachers who are informed of these concepts gain a deeper appreciation and understanding of the importance their role plays in the faith development of children.

MULTIPLE INTELLIGENCES

The study of multiple intelligences defines what we already intuitively know—children learn in many different ways. Children are not identical, and we cannot take a cookie-cutter approach to Christian education. Some children love coloring Bible pictures, and others jump at the opportunity to be in a skit. Great curricula offer a variety of learning experiences; great teachers provide these even if the curriculum lacks creativity.

Dr. Howard Gardner's original seven intelligences have grown to nine today. Memorizing each one is less important than appreciating God's creative variety and striving to accommodate these differences while teaching. But for the record, the nine styles/pathways/intelligences to learning are as follows: word smart (linguistic intelligence), math smart (logical-mathematical intelligence), music smart (musical intelligence), picture smart (spatial intelligence), body smart (bodily-kinesthetic intelligence), people smart (interpersonal intelligence), self-smart (intrapersonal intelligence), nature smart (naturalist intelligence), and life smart (existential intelligence). As teachers incorporate many different activities and experiences in their lessons, they reach children with varying learning styles.

SPECIAL NEEDS

Children are not one size fits all! Boys and girls with Down syndrome, communication difficulties, physical limitations, autism spectrum disorder, or learning disabilities create unique challenges for teachers. Our call is to bring Jesus' love to each and every child; thus, staff may need to be equipped to handle unique situations.

Because parents want their children to be well cared for, they are the first place to go to gain information. Ask candid questions about their child's abilities or disabilities and about what works and what doesn't. Your sincere interest and care will benefit you as you teach and the student as he or she learns. In addition, you may want to investigate additional resources or seek further advice from special education teachers to gain more information and suggestions on how best to serve the child's unique needs.

As an aside, not everyone has the necessary qualities to work well with children who have unique needs. These individuals usually have a matter-of-fact approach to life. They express empathy but not pity. They show kindness without fawning. A person with these qualities will invite confidence and trust from students and parents alike.

DISCIPLINE

When I first started teaching, I naively thought that providing relevant and creative lessons for my first and second graders would eliminate misbehavior in our classroom. Was I in for a surprise! Innovative teaching is a good start, but in reality, the old Adam is alive and well in all of us regardless of age.

Setting limits for children is essential in providing a safe and happy place for all to learn and grow. *Discipline* comes from the root word *disciple*. The Scriptures make it clear that discipline is an integral part of the life of a disciple of Jesus. When we take the time to carefully guide the behavior of children, we are helping them understand how a Christ-follower lives and relates to others.

Two key facets of classroom discipline are prevention and intervention. Let's begin with an overview of prevention in order to prepare before potential problems arise.

Prevention

Preventative discipline means anticipating what could go wrong and planning how to keep that from happening in the first place. One fundamental factor is simply providing ample classroom assistance so teachers can focus on the lesson, confident that support staff will help keep children attentive.

Adequate lesson preparation is also foundational. It enables the teacher to know the material well enough to focus on the children and maintain eye contact rather than merely reading the script. Part of the planning process that will help keep the attention of kids is ensuring that lessons are age appropriate and creative. A message too babyish, too complex, or too boring seems to give children the license to disengage and find more interesting things to do that rarely fit the teacher's agenda. The time of preparation must include anticipating how to assist the children in smoothly transitioning from one activity to another. Imagining it first prepares the way for its actual occurrence.

There's a saying that class begins when the first child enters the room. This holds true whether the teacher is ready or not. Therefore, arriving early to get materials and supplies set out and organized is critical. It's a rare child that will patiently and quietly wait while teachers gather their stuff and prepare the room.

One reality we must face is how some children have the uncanny ability to trigger strong emotional reactions within us. A child's behavior may spark a surge of anger or a desire to keep one's distance. We may recognize the temptation to respond in ways that do not represent Jesus well. Part of preventative discipline is seeking God's help to deal with these inner personal responses before class begins. Ask God to shine His light of understanding in your heart so you can identify the source of both your reaction and the child's behavior. Ask Him to exchange your resentment for His grace and mercy. Children will be more open to hear truth from teachers who like and understand them.

This fact occurred to me earlier this week in the pool. My husband and I are regulars at our local fitness club's Aqua Fit classes. Over time, instructors and substitutes come and go. When we as a class sense that the instructor likes us, we work hard and have fun. An indifferent or ill-tempered coach generates eye-rolling and grumpiness—not a pretty picture for adults!

Take the time to get to know the children. Find out their likes and dislikes; ask about their families, pets, schools, and interests. Josh McDowell coined the saying that "rules without relationship leads to rebellion." Few positive outcomes will occur spiritually and emotionally without a companionable relationship.

Speaking of rules, it's important to have them and for children to know them. Allow me to offer a suggestion even though it may be tricky to remember. Rather than stating rules in the negative, such as "don't run," try expressing what you *do* want the children to do instead, such as "walk your shoes." This variation may be subtle, but offering more positive statements helps create a more concrete picture of what is appropriate. It changes the teacher's role from being a policeman who spots infractions to a coach who guides behavior. For young children, you may include rules such as these: listen to what your teachers say; say nice, kind, and loving things; hands and feet do nice, kind, and loving things; take turns; our hands stay on our own body. For older children, you may include these: respect others; follow directions; listen; make good choices. Create the rules that work best for you and your particular group of children. Be sure to keep them few and easy to remember.

Intervention

Intervening discipline means handling misconduct when it occurs. Because we live in a fallen world, kids choosing to act up should not come as a surprise. When these incidents are minor, teachers can respond indirectly. Here are some examples.

» Call attention to positive examples of children complying. "I like the way Billy and Joey are putting away their toys." (Note that this is far different from making comparisons such as "Why can't you put away your toys like Billy and Joey?")

» Walk toward the student or stand close to him or her.

» Signal to a child using eye contact, a smile, a wink, a head nod, or by shaking your head no.

» Insert a child's name in the Bible story or conversation. "Do you know what Jesus did next, Julie? He told the disciples He wanted the kids to come to Him!"

» Touch a child on the shoulder.

» Ask a child to do a simple task for you that will make him or her feel important.

» Redirect a young child to another area of play.

Sometimes kids need a more direct approach. Volunteer teachers have told me about their reluctance to discipline for fear that the child will not want to return to church. But a misbehaving child is not a happy child, and neither are the other children who have to put up with such mischief. Some of the following suggestions may be helpful.

» Use the child's name to refocus his or her attention. "Jimmy, eyes and ears up here, please."

» Give a positive direct instruction. "It's time to listen quietly now. You may talk when the story is over."

» Use an "I" message. "Jenny, I need you to sit down so I'm not distracted."

» Whisper a request to a child.

» Provide choices, but only those that are acceptable to you. "Would you rather sit by your friend without touching him or sit next to me?"

» Provide a time-out for students or a no-fun chair for little ones who may need to regain control. "Julie, you can sit in this chair for a couple minutes, and then we can talk."

» Say what *you* will do. "I give snacks to children who treat their projects well." The Love and Logic technique calls this an enforceable statement (see next paragraph).

» Ask your director or supervisor for advice on dealing with a situation.

Love and Logic is a tool that many schools and churches turn to for help with discipline (www.loveandlogic.com). How I wish I had known the concepts of enforceable statements, offering choices, and showing empathy without anger when my children were young! I highly recommend checking out their website, conferences, books, and audio resources, all of which offer practical assistance to both teachers and parents.

Your staff also needs to know what responses on their part are *not* allowed for a child's misbehavior. Here is a list with which to start.

» Placing a child in the hall

» Spanking, shaking, or yanking

» Saying or doing anything to embarrass or degrade a child

» Telling a child he or she is bad

» Making idle threats with no follow-up

» Raising your voice

» Using God's name in vain

Finally, make it clear to your staff how and by whom parents are to be notified. I encouraged my staff to talk with me before initiating a conversation with parents regarding discipline concerns. Moms and dads of children who get in trouble frequently at school need encouragement rather than more evidence of misbehavior in church. "Tattling" to a parent is rarely beneficial for them or their children. Empathetically supporting them and brainstorming together how their child can be guided as a disciple of Jesus reaps eternal rewards.

* * * *

Ten years ago I was a small-group leader in a very large church. One Sunday, a sweet and shy little girl was brought to my table. Our spirits connected. She stayed after class with her parents and little sister, and we got to know one another a little better. Week by week, this relationship grew. As trust was established in the years ahead, Taylor's parents allowed us to have outings, and the bond was strengthened. We now consider each other family, and I simply introduce Taylor and Ashley as my nieces. God took my offering of time and turned it into a beautiful relationship. God always gives the better thing.

Carol Zachrich
Woodside Bible Church
Romeo, MI

* * * *

One child I worked with was having some severe behavioral issues that could not be resolved in the past. After many positive and negative sanctions, no behavioral change happened. It turned out the adults working with the child were only responding to the symptoms but not addressing the issue. The child was actually experiencing a lot of hurt in his life and no one bothered to ask why. The battles children can face have no limits and require time to listen, to care, and to have wisdom to make the right professional decisions in the face of difficult situations.

Kyle McCall
Graduate, Concordia University Texas
Austin, Texas

* * * *

Age-Level Characteristics

Age	Physical Characteristics	Social, Behavioral, Emotional Characteristics	What We Want Children to Know & Experience Spiritually
Infant–Toddler	Depends on adults to meet all needs Imitates actions Uses senses to explore Learns to crawl & walk	Shows rapid growth Cries to communicate needs Recognizes & learns simple words Requires loving, consistent caregivers to build trust	I (parent, caretaker) love you I (parent, caretaker) take care of you God made me Jesus loves me too
2–3	Walks, climbs, feeds self Makes progress with potty-training Builds towers, throws balls, paints, turns pages of books Scribbles & learns to cut a straight line	Follows one direction at a time May fear leaving parents Says "No!" and "Me do it!" Plays alone Finds sharing & taking turns hard Requires concrete vocabulary Has a 2–3+ minute attention span	God made the world I am God's child Jesus came as a baby Jesus is my friend The Bible is a special book I can pray to God
4–5	Shows improvement in large- & small-muscle coordination Cuts large objects, begins to color in the lines Draws recognizable objects Learns to write own name	Participates in group activities Asks "Why?" "How?" "What?" Loves imaginative play Learns to share Has a 4–5+ minute attention span	Jesus is God's Son Jesus died for our sins Jesus rose from the dead & is still alive I can talk to God about anything God takes care of me Jesus wants me to be kind God's Word is true I can pray the Lord's Prayer

Age	Physical Characteristics	Social, Behavioral, Emotional Characteristics	What We Want Children to Know & Experience Spiritually
6–7	Shows more improvement in small-muscle coordination Learns to read & write Seeks personal attention Girls develop faster than boys	Places more importance on friends Wants to help adults Has a 6–7+ minute attention span	I recognize my sin & know Jesus forgives me Baptism is a sign that I belong to God God helps me obey There are three parts to God The Old Testament happened before Jesus' birth I can say the books of the Bible
8–9	Shows good large- & small-muscle coordination Reads with more confidence	Prefers activities with same sex Gives or receives peer teasing Depends less on adults Has a 8–9+ minute attention span	I understand my need for a Savior A Christian believes in Jesus as Savior I can say the 10 Commandments I became God's child in Baptism
10–11	Masters physical skills Reads well unless displays a disability Girls may start to experience physical changes	Becomes more self-conscious Values peer acceptance Reasons more abstractly Begins to question beliefs Has a 10–11+ minute attention span	The Bible relates to my own life God talks to me through His Word Faiths saves, not works I can tell others about Jesus It is safe to trust God I can have my own daily devotions I can arrange events in Bible history I can say the Apostles' Creed

Multiple Intelligences: How Teachers Can Engage Children through Their Learning Styles

Multiple Intelligence	Description	Activities That Engage Children through Their Personal Learning Styles
Word smart (linguistic intelligence)	Learn with words and value the use of language	Read Scripture, skits Write stories, poems, journal, newsletters Discussions, interviews Listen to stories
Math smart (logical-mathematical intelligence)	Think with logic and order and are aware of cause and effect	Explore solutions Consider thinking questions Bible computer games Express rationale
Music smart (musical intelligence)	Love rhythm, sounds, melodies, and rhymes	Sing Beats and tunes that teach Play instruments Background music
Picture smart (spatial intelligence)	Use their imagination and think in pictures	Visual aids Crafts, projects Displays of pictures, art Biblical maps
Body smart (bodily-kinesthetic intelligence)	Learn best through moving and touching	Teach Bible stories with movement Drama, role play Objects to touch Crafts, projects

Multiple Intelligence	Description	Activities That Engage Children through Their Personal Learning Styles
People smart (interpersonal intelligence)	Aware of other people and how they interact together	Discussion in pairs, triads Get acquainted activities Parties, celebrations
Self smart (intrapersonal intelligence)	Know themselves well and think about human nature	Independent activities Personal prayer, reflection One-on-one conversations
Nature smart (naturalist intelligence)	Aware of and appreciate the natural world	Scripture references to nature Lessons held outdoors, walks Classroom windows with beautiful view Care for God's creation
Life smart (existential intelligence)	Desire to examine deep questions about the meaning of life	Biblical life application Guide child in leadership Point out learning connections Explore lives of Christ-followers

Special Needs

WORKING WITH FAMILIES WITH CHILDREN WHO HAVE SPECIAL NEEDS

	Attention Difficulties—ADD/ADHD	Autism Spectrum Disorders	Learning Disabilities
Signs	Easily distracted by self or others Difficulty with organization Inattentive to details Difficulty finishing or remembering tasks Difficulty waiting turn/frequently interrupts Fidgets/has trouble remaining in seat or focusing on one task for a long period of time Difficulty with transitions	Difficulty relating to peers Unusual play with toys and other objects Difficulty with changes in routine or familiar surroundings Repetitive body movements, behaviors, and language Difficulty using and understanding language/communication	Reading, writing, and spelling skills significantly lower than peers Speak in short, concrete sentences Difficulty remembering which word to use Trouble with activities requiring sequencing of steps May appear noncompliant due to not understanding rules or directions May act out to avoid reading and writing tasks
Strengths	Creative Energetic Able to think outside the box Average or above-average intelligence Friendly	Intense area of interest IQ in average to superior range Specific interests can be avenue to learning Strong rote memory skills	Average or above-average intelligence Creative May be very good at right-brained tasks (arts, sports, etc.) Learn by doing/hands-on activities

	Attention Difficul- ties—ADD/ADHD	Autism Spectrum Disorders	Learning Disabilities
Struggles	Maintaining attention Sitting still Remembering details Following directions Compliance with rules or social norms	Communicating wants and needs Social interactions with peers Transitions and lack of routine Possible sensitivity to specific sounds, foods, clothing Possible language, academic, and developmental delays Abstract concepts and com- prehension Inappropriate behavior when unable to communicate	Reading and writing activities Understanding abstract concepts Following multistep directions Maintaining attention Memory
Strategies	Minimize distractions and noise Establish clear expectations and limits Use positive reinforcement and logical consequences Use visuals as reminders rather than talking Give written directions as well as verbal Include movement in lessons Change activities every 5–10 minutes Call student's name before asking question Allow student to stand or walk in back of room away from others Use stress balls/tactile objects	Provide highly structured and predictable routines Use visual schedules Understand and minimize behavior triggers Invite parents to come on Saturday for a practice session Find quiet place for student to go when needed Provide positive feedback Explain to the class that God made each person different	Reduce memory work or writing associated with it Present information in smaller amounts Use lower reading level Bible and materials Use recorded Bible stories Allow students to dictate responses Use computer for written responses Give written directions as well as verbal Keep lessons short and to the point Include movement in lessons, especially to remember sequences Emphasize the student's successes

Permission granted from Lutheran Special Education Ministries (www.luthsped.org)

Discipline Self-Evaluation for Teachers

Read chapter 8 and reflect on the following questions.

1. Prevention—Preventative discipline means anticipating what could go wrong and planning how to keep misconduct from occurring in the first place.

   a. Does my support staff help keep the children attentive during the lesson?

   b. Do I know my material well enough to maintain eye contact with the children?

   c. Is my material age appropriate and interesting?

   d. Do my transitions from one activity to another run smoothly?

   e. Am I prepared for class? Are my materials and my room prepared when the first child arrives?

   f. Do I like each of the children in my class? Have I sorted out my adverse feelings with God?

   g. How have I taken the initiative to get to know each of the children?

   h. What are my classroom rules?

   i. Are they clear? Are they stated positively?

2. Intervention—Intervening discipline means handling misconduct when it occurs.

   a. Which of the following indirect ideas from chapter 8 could be helpful for you when dealing with minor infractions?

   • Call attention to positive examples of children complying.

   • Walk toward the student or stand close to him or her.

   • Signal to a child using eye contact, a smile, a wink, a head nod, or by shaking your head no.

- Insert a child's name in the Bible story or conversation.
- Touch a child on the shoulder.
- Ask a child to do a simple task for you that will make him or her feel important.

b. Which of the following ideas could benefit you when you need a more direct approach?

- Use the child's name to refocus attention.
- Give a positive direct instruction.
- Use an "I" message.
- Whisper a request to a child.
- Redirect a young child to another area of play.
- Provide choices, but only those that are acceptable to you.
- Provide a time-out for students or a no-fun chair for little ones who may need to regain control.
- Say what *you* will do.
- Ask your director/supervisor for advice on dealing with a situation.

What Do I Need to Know about Administration?

"Now you are the body of Christ and individually members of it. And God has appointed in the church . . . gifts of . . . administrating . . . . And I will show you a still more excellent way." 1 Corinthians 12:27–28, 31b

Knowing how to lead a well-run organization is truly a gift from God. But knowing how to administer a program with *God's love* front and center is "still more excellent," to use Paul's words. It is easy to get so caught up in the whirlwind of completing tasks that we lose sight of the foundational purpose undergirding those tasks in the first place. None of the administrative tasks mentioned in this chapter are to be done simply for the sake of doing them. The greater goal is to bring glory to God and carry out the mission to which you have been called.

LEADING MEETINGS

Meetings are inevitable, and there may be lots of them! I've heard people say, "I could get a lot more work done if it weren't for meetings!" You'll be the first to agree with that assessment if you've ever been in a discussion that goes on forever and accomplishes little. Let's talk about preparing meetings that achieve results so people feel their time has not been wasted. Where to start? At the beginning, of course.

Before the meeting:

- » Clarify the purpose of your meeting. Be able to fill in the blank: At the end of the meeting, I hope _____.

- » Prayerfully think through all the items that require discussion, and then create your agenda.

- » Consider how you will balance the need to address tasks and the need to build relationships on your team.

- » Keep the agenda realistic and as short as possible. Take care of as many tasks as you can before the meeting to lessen the time needed.

- » Be sure people know the time allotted for the meeting, so they won't be constantly watching the clock.

- » Identify "owners" of topics and make sure they know your expectations.

- » You may also want to allocate time limits for each agenda item to keep things moving.

- » Decide who needs to attend the meeting. Each person there needs to play a role. Should the attendees be your regular team, key decision-makers, people affected by the decision, or people with helpful information? For decision-making purposes, a group of four to seven people is ideal.

- » Schedule the meeting; if needed, make sure the room is reserved.

- » Send out your agenda. Include brief supporting materials if needed. It is perfectly okay to ask participants to come prepared with ideas or solutions. The more they invest in the agenda ahead of time, the more thorough the discussion.

- » Arrive early to arrange the room for easy conversation. Gather and prepare any needed supplies. I prefer a circle for small groups and a U shape of chairs or tables for a midsize group.

During the meeting:

» Start on time. Resist the temptation to recap for latecomers; hopefully this omission will encourage them to be more prompt next time.

» Identify a notetaker if you wish it to be someone other than yourself. Decisions need to be documented to prevent later misunderstanding.

» Identify your goals and review the agenda. Ask for any additions.

» Keep the group on task. One of the biggest challenges is keeping people focused on the subject matter. Maybe you want to create your own lingo for the tendency to wander, such as "getting in the weeds" or "going down a rabbit hole." When someone gets off task, the others in the group *want* the leader to get back on target so the meeting isn't prolonged. If someone offers an idea that is off subject, jot it down in the "parking lot," a list of items for later discussion.

» Encourage full participation. You may want to go around the room and ask each person to express his or her opinion on a matter.

» If you decide to brainstorm, write down all the suggestions offered. Only allow critique and discussion after all ideas have been exhausted.

» To more fully explore a controversial topic or to make meetings more fun, you could ask people to assume specific roles, such as devil's advocate, timekeeper, or parking-lot writer.

» Watch the body language of the people in your group. If someone is glassy-eyed, how can you liven things up or bring that person back to the discussion? If people are getting fidgety, maybe it's time for a break or a sign you need to curtail someone who is monopolizing the conversation.

» If you detect tension, expose any elephants in the room. You could say something like, "I'm feeling some tension right now. Is there something we should be talking about?"

» Embrace silence and don't feel like you need to fill every moment. People need time to think, especially the introverts.

» Avoid groupthink. Expressing a variety of opinions is not only beneficial but also needful. It's unrealistic to think that all people will have the same opinion on every matter. Thank people for their courage when they express a different view.

» Hold participants to high standards of courtesy. Unfortunately, even in a church setting, one cannot assume manners will always be displayed.

» Make sure people know how decisions will be made. Methods may vary for the issue at hand. Will the leader make the final decision? Will the group take a vote and expect 100-percent agreement before an idea can move forward? Will the group arrive at a consensus where everyone agrees to support the final decision even though it may not be their first choice? Will you lead the team in praying for discernment and a focus on God's will?

» Verbally summarize any decision reached.

» Agree on an action plan. Clarify the point person, tasks others will assume, and the dates by which they need to be completed.

» Confirm the date for the next meeting and ask for agenda items.

» Close on time.

» You may want to occasionally request feedback from participants on their perception of the effectiveness of the meetings. Give them the opportunity to express strengths, weaknesses, and ideas that could enhance your time together.

After the meeting:

» Distribute and archive the minutes. These don't need to be formal, but they do need to identify decisions made, people assuming responsibility for certain tasks, and designated timelines. Taking notes on the original agenda is even acceptable as long as they are copied and given to the participants.

» Review the high and low points of the meeting; acknowledge what went well and learn from your mistakes.

» Follow up on actions required by specified point people.

» Prepare for the next meeting.

I am one of those rare birds who loves leading meetings—usually. Following the above-mentioned suggestions invites people into a rewarding partnership to explore what God is unfolding in your faith community.

CALENDARIZING

Give me a fresh, new calendar at the beginning of the year, and I'm one happy gal. (I know, I need to get a life!) Planning strategically makes the plans God set and placed in your heart a reality. It gives you goals to move toward. Once items are placed on a calendar, it puts legs on events that were mere ideas days before. The calendar enables you to plan ahead and anticipate crunch times. It helps you pray about setting priorities.

If you are new to ministry, give yourself a year to learn the ebb and flow in the cycle of the Church Year and its related activities. Even though the Church Year officially begins with Advent, because the school year is so deeply ingrained in my life, I more naturally see September as the start of the ministry season. This means that spring is the time to hold a planning retreat with your team to look at the entire school year that lies ahead.

Go back to the beginning with your V/P/M statement. This is your foundation in planning. Anything that comes up for discussion that does not support this basis can be eliminated immediately. When preparing a children's ministry church calendar, I follow these steps:

1. Write in the church festivals first—Thanksgiving, Christmas, Ash Wednesday, Easter, etc.

2. Get your local school calendar and note the beginning and end of school as well as all the vacation days during the year. An event planned near a school vacation could limit those able to attend.

3. Write in the major ongoing church programs, such as these:

   a. Church events that have already been scheduled on the master calendar like the annual church picnic.

   b. Sunday School. Are there any Sundays you won't meet? What happens in the summer? If you meet all year, when will you transition kids to the next grade?

   c. Midweek classes. Having church festivals and school holidays already calendarized will help you select the dates to meet.

   d. Special events based on the time of year, such as VBS, the Christmas program, or an Easter fair. Are these scheduled in such a way that you can encourage guests to attend upcoming events?

   e. Child care. Do you need to provide childcare for special worship services or events?

   f. Volunteer training or appreciation. How do you plan to prepare and appreciate your staff?

   g. Parenting classes, Baptisms, stepping stones. If serving parents is part of your ministry or mission, how will you support them this year?

4. Consider new events. This is the time to prayerfully talk with your team about all those ideas that people throw out from time to time that you have hopefully been jotting down in the parking lot—things like sports camp, scouts, singing in church, game night, creating Thanksgiving baskets, or the one-day VBS during spring break. The temptation to do too much is great, so if you add a new activity this year, be sure you have the time, energy, and manpower to do so. Don't be afraid to say no.

Once your calendar is established, share it with everyone you can—church leadership, parents, volunteers. Communication is so important that I have devoted chapter 11 solely to that topic.

ATTENDANCE

Keeping attendance records and following up on absentees prevents anyone at your church from having an out of sight, out of mind experience. What a privilege to show personal care by encouraging kids and their parents to stay connected to the body of believers! It's an opportunity to assume the role of spiritual shepherd and reach out with Jesus' love. I'm undoubtedly in the minority, but I *love* calling families who don't attend church for a while.

Most church leaders are not quite as eager to make calls of this nature. Ministry is already busy, for goodness' sake! And people might respond in not-so-nice ways. Who wants to experience a cold reception or worse?

To be honest, I only recall one unpleasant call from the thousands I have made through the years. Yes, some people don't answer the phone and others are complacent. But other individuals use that moment to convey a circumstance in their lives, such as revealing an illness or a child who couldn't make friends at church or even admitting to "church shopping." Many people do express their appreciation for the encouragement to become more faithful in worship.

My calls simply begin with, "Hello, I'm Cynthia Brown, and I work with children at _____ Lutheran Church. We've missed seeing your kids in Sunday School and are wondering if there is something we can do to encourage them to return." Then it's time to listen and respond with grace as the Holy Spirit leads.

GUESTS

We can only follow up on attendance if we have initially done our homework and gathered contact information when people first enter the door as a guest. Most people agree to share their address in order to receive church mailings for special events. Our desire is to encourage infrequent guests to participate in regular discipleship opportunities. Be sure you have a plan in place to encourage ongoing spiritual growth. It often takes many contacts over a number of years for a family to think of your church body as their spiritual home.

Consider giving guests a gift bag that may simply consist of a welcome note from you, a children's ministry brochure, and candy or a small book or puzzle. You may also want to mail a welcome postcard to a visiting child or family; receiving personal mail is a rarity these days for anyone!

First impressions are important and determine whether a guest will return. I prefer using the term *guest* rather than *visitor* because the former infers the warmth we would extend when a friend arrives at our home. When we remember that Jesus resides within our faith community, we will want to extend His love to all who enter His home as well.

And when guests take the next step and become regulars, I love to make welcome calls to their families. Those five minutes of conversation extend a warm, personal welcome and invite opportunities to answer questions.

The call is as simple as "Hello, I'm Cynthia Brown, and I direct the children's ministry at _____ Lutheran Church. I received your children's registration form and simply wanted to call and say 'Welcome.' How have your children been adjusting to their new classes?" During the conversation I may also ask, "How did you first become acquainted with our church?" These phone calls have provided rich opportunities to build new relationships with families and to relay information about upcoming events.

BUDGETING

Handling finances is probably my least favorite administrative task; I would rather clean the sinks. During a particularly frustrating moment in high school when my mother was trying to teach me how to balance a checkbook, she exclaimed, "You need to marry a banker to do this for you!" To her relief, my husband did go into banking a few years after we married. But that didn't help me much at church, where I had to figure out financial details by myself.

Churches have different approaches to dealing with the budget, so it's important to learn all you can about your organization's practices. To begin with, identify your church's fiscal year. Is it the same as the calendar year, or does it start midsummer or in the fall? Second, ask your treasurer for a list of all the expenditures for the previous year to give you a baseline for the new season of ministry. Find out what happens to the kids' Sunday School offerings or to the VBS registration fees. Ask whether children's ministry has any self-funding programs, such as preschool, VBS, or sports, and compare the income and expenses. Learn all you can about how money flows in and out of the accounts.

Small churches may have a single line item for children's ministry. Even if this is the case, you will want to know specific amounts allocated for curriculum or classroom supplies or the Christmas program. Facts about expenditures and income immediately reveal your ministry priorities. They can help you evaluate whether programs or events should continue the following year or whether resources are available to support new ministry endeavors.

Churches with larger budgets may subdivide children's ministry into various categories. Choose whatever method will best enable you to make decisions for the present and plan for the future. One option is to subdivide the ministry budget into age categories, such as nursery, preschool, and elementary children. This approach allows you to see how much money is allocated per child in each age range. A second option is to identify the different programs within your children's ministry, such as Sunday School, VBS, choir, or sports. This method immediately shows you total costs for each program. A third option is to create general expense categories—such as equipment, publicity, curriculum, or training—and consolidate expenses for all the events and programs. These expense categories can also be added to the first two options mentioned above.

Your budget needs to reflect your V/P/M and goals. For example, if you determine to partner with parents as they teach the faith to their children, financial resources must exist to support this effort. Of course, all budgets need to be approved by the voters. Deliberate and prayerful planning will prepare you to give account for the funds requested for the new fiscal year.

FACILITIES

As I begin this section, I am sensitive toward churches that struggle financially. As membership decreases in many churches, resources become fewer. Some city churches in our area even rely on the generosity of congregations in the suburbs. Facilities are important—we will look at reasons why—but other attributes take precedence. Friends have told me stories of their astonishment at the joy of children and the generosity of people living in complete squalor in other parts of the world. An addendum to 1 Corinthians 13 might include, "If I had the most beautiful children's facility in all the world, but did not communicate God's love, it is a clanging gong." Regardless of how we can afford to decorate our children's areas, we want to express God's love so children and parents feel welcome the moment they enter His house.

Walk into a church for the first time, and you can immediately tell how members regard the children in their congregation. First impressions say a great deal about what a church deems important. According to Thom Rainer in *Surprising Insights from the Unchurched* (Grand Rapids: Zondervan, 2001), the top five factors that are most important to the unchurched when they eventually decide to visit a church are genuine friendliness of members; clean church facilities and adequate space; specifically, the cleanliness, neatness, and safety of the children's spaces; an overall sense of organization or chaos; and the presence of greeters and welcome centers.

Please do not be tempted to dismiss these factors as invalid because they are not very "spiritual" reasons to attend church. The perspectives of outsiders can be far different from our own. We want to do all we can to prevent anything from standing in the way of folks hearing the Gospel. Having well-ordered facilities is not about us; it's paving the way for people to be open to receiving all God has in store for them.

To begin the evaluation process, ask several parents to walk through your children's area with you. Those who do not attend your church would probably offer a more objective perspective; it's hard to see our own environment with fresh eyes. Ask them to critique what they see and to comment on attractiveness, modernization, safety, and cleanliness. Consider this checklist as you scrutinize the facilities:

» Entrance—Does the welcome/informational area provide guests with the information they need?

» Hallways, walls, ceilings, floors—Are these areas clean and attractive?

» Restrooms—Are they clean enough for your loved ones to use? Are changing tables located in both men and women's rooms? Are there stools for washing little hands?

» Cry room—Is it clean and stocked with a changing table, rockers, quiet toys, Bibles, and bulletins?

» Classrooms—Are they clean, organized, and attractive? Will kids want to play with the toys and games? Is there storage for teaching materials, technology, first-aid kits, snacks, and cleaning supplies? Do you see a picture of Jesus?

» Nursery—Does it look and smell fresh? Is it supplied with a changing table, safe toys, and infant furniture like swings and infant seats?

» Resource room—Do the teachers and staff have a well-organized area for supplies and crafts?

» Safety—Is the building prepped for safety? Are the areas for the littlest ones childproofed? Do you see CPR charts or directions for emergency evacuation? Is an AED available?

Once you have a realistic picture of your environment, form a plan to spruce it up. Look at church websites and visit other churches to stimulate your imagination. Doing so may momentarily stir up covetous feelings, so check yourself and remember to ask God to clarify *His* desires for your setting. Create a written proposal and realistic timeline for the changes you hope to enact.

An overhaul does not need to break the bank. Consider some of the following thrifty resources that may already be at your disposal:

» Funds in your church budget—Be sure to use the money that has already been allocated.

» Custodians—Build a relationship with these underappreciated men and women, who are usually told about messes and not given words of appreciation. He or she might be willing to do a special favor for you if you need help improving an area.

» Decor—People who like to decorate their homes might be willing to serve on a task force and offer suggestions for redecorating your children's area. Perhaps a resident artist would be willing to paint murals on the walls or guide volunteers to do so.

» Volunteer labor—If you share your vision clearly, people will step up to help realize those dreams. Volunteers can paint, repair, build, sew, install, and clean. Be sure to honor the time they spend with some form of appreciation.

» Other churches—Churches with more resources may be willing to share their unneeded supplies, games, or toys with you. They may even be willing to adopt a special mission project and share their offerings with your church. Requests can be made through district newsletters.

» Discretionary funds—Pastors often have funds to use for special needs or projects. Perhaps he would be willing to share some resources with you for a specific item or project.

» New and gently used donations—As parents breathe a sigh of relief that their kids' playrooms are being purged, you can rejoice at the new items that grace your closets at church.

» Garage sales or rummage sales—You or your designated shoppers can delight in finding bargains to equip your nursery or classrooms.

» Gift registry—Did you know that churches can create registries? People are happy to use their offerings to purchase items that they know will be put to good use at church. Some Christian publishers even have registries for resources.

» Fund-raiser—If your church allows fund-raisers, you may want to use the profits toward your facility goals.

If your church has a Day School or preschool, classrooms are probably shared between ministries. It doesn't take long for a frustrated teacher who finds supplies missing to start protecting his or her turf. Holding out a vision for cooperation between ministry staffs is imperative. When there is consistent communication and a desire for Christlike attitudes, I have seen a church move from locked cupboards for "my stuff" to generously sharing all resources. This is heart transformation!

DELEGATION

There's so much to do! Opportunities, tasks, and issues are never ending. Jesus experienced people clamoring after Him all day long, and His response amazes me. At times, He continued with His work; at other times, He left the crowds and traveled elsewhere. It would have been humanly impossible to meet every single need of every single person, and it would have been unwise.

Jesus' constant communion with His heavenly Father gave Him the clarity to decide where to put His efforts each and every day. As the Son of God, He perfectly knew His mission; He knew what to let go of and what to focus on. During His short ministry period, He accomplished what only He could do, and He prepared others to carry the mission forward after His absence.

In *Management for the Christian Leader*, author Olan Hendrix credits Peter Drucker with his three diagnostic questions for the effective management of time.

1. What am I doing that really does not need to be done by me or anyone else?

2. Which of the activities on my time log could be handled as well, if not better, by someone else?

3. What do I do that wastes the other people's time?

He suggests that it is important for leaders to learn "how to identify the work that we are doing and [devise] methods of passing these pieces of work on to other people, but [maintain] a management check on these activities."[14] I think that is what Jesus was doing in Luke 10 when He heard the reports of the seventy-two disciples He sent out two by two to teach and to heal.

Delegation takes time and patience; sometimes it's easier to complete the task ourselves. Delegating to others requires a willingness to offer the limelight to them. It requires humility in knowing that another person might be able to do the task better than we can do it ourselves. It requires trust that "their way" of undertaking the assignment might be different from "my way" and still be acceptable. This generosity of heart is the way of Jesus.

---

14 Olan Hendrix, *Management for the Christian Leader* (Grand Rapids: Baker, 1988), 90.

Sample Meeting Agenda

Group Name_____

Date_____

Time_____

Location_____

Current Purpose/Vision/Mission Statement

1. Prayer and Discussion: How is God working in your life since we last met?

2. A look back . . .

3. A look at the present . . .

4. A look ahead . . .

5. What else?

6. Next meeting

   Parking-Lot Ideas:

   _____

   _____

   _____

   _____

Sample Registration Card

FaithKids Registration 2015-2016

Date: _____

Register for: ☐ **Sunday Morning**   ☐ **Wednesday Night**

CHILD INFORMATION:

Child's Name _____

Child's Address/City/Zip _____

Home Phone _____

Child's DOB _____ Gender _____ Age or Grade _____

Allergies _____

Has your child been baptized?   ☐ Yes   ☐ No

- -

PARENT INFORMATION:

Child's Mother _____

Child's Father _____

Parent Cell Phone(s) _____

Email _____

- -

☐   I AM INTERESTED IN VOLUNTEER OPPORTUNITIES IN CHILDREN'S MINISTRY.

☐   I AM INTERESTED IN RECEIVING MONTHLY "PARENT LINK" NEWSLETTER VIA EMAIL.

Name _____

- -

◆ ***ALTERNATE PICKUP:*** Please list names of person(s) your child can be released to *(in addition to mother and father)*:

_____   _____

◆ ***EMERGENCY CONTACT(S):*** If parents cannot be reached:

Name_____   Phone_____

Name_____   Phone_____

- -

◆ **Other *SPECIAL CIRCUMSTANCES*** we should be aware of to better minister to your child: (health issues, someone other than parents bringing child, etc.)

_____

Sample Guest Card

FaithKids Guest Information Card

Today's Date:
—2015

Child's First & Last Name (Please print)   **Grade** or **Age**

_____ _____ _____

_____ _____ _____

_____ _____ _____

_____ _____ _____

<u>I have visited Sunday or Wednesday FaithKids before.</u> ☐ *(Check box, skip rest of form.)*

Child's Address_____

(This information will be used only to send welcome card to child)

Email _____

(Optional)

Phones _____ _____ _____

(Optional) **Home**   **Mom's Cell**   **Dad's Cell**

Please call me with more information about children's ministry at Faith:

Name_____**Phone #**_____

Something to Noodle about . . . What's Next?

» If an unchurched guest attends your VBS program, how will you encourage his or her spiritual growth—What's next?

» If a guest family attends your Christmas family event, how will you encourage ongoing spiritual growth—What's next?

Facilities Checklist

» **Entrance**—Does the welcome/informational area provide guests with the information they need?

» **Hallways, walls, ceilings, floors**—Are these areas clean and attractive? Are hallways unobstructed? Does the paint appear fresh? Is the flooring unsoiled? Can children reach the drinking fountains? Are there clear direction signs?

» **Restrooms**—Are they clean enough for your loved ones to use? Do they look attractive? Are changing tables located in both men and women's rooms? Are there stools for washing little hands?

» **Cry room**—Does it look clean and smell fresh? Is the worship service visible or audible to parents? Is the room stocked with a changing table, rockers, quiet toys, Bibles, and bulletins? Do you see a picture of Jesus?

» **Nursery**—Does it look clean and smell fresh? Is it supplied with a changing table, safe toys, and infant furniture like swings and infant seats? Are outlet safety covers inserted and sharp corners padded? Is there a means to contact parents should the need arise? Are cubbies available for personal belongings? Is there a one-way window to allow for parent viewing? Do you see a picture of Jesus?

» **Classrooms**—Are they clean, organized, and attractive? Is the furniture sized to the children and in good condition? Is the room sized to the number of children? Will kids want to play with the toys and games? Are there adequate supplies for each child? Is there storage for teaching materials, technology, first-aid kits, snacks, and cleaning supplies? Do the rooms have two doors allowing for safe check-in and check-out procedures? Do rooms have windows or half doors to allow for parent viewing? Is tech equipment adequate? Do you see a picture of Jesus?

» **Resource room**—Do the teachers and staff have a well-organized area for supplies and crafts? Is it well stocked? Is there a work area for projects? Is there a process for checking out materials or resources?

» **Safety**—Is the building prepped for safety? Are evacuation procedures posted in each room? Are the areas for the littlest ones childproofed? Does each room have a first-aid kit and CPR charts? Is an AED available?

Next Steps to Address Facility Needs

1.

2.

3.

How Do I Prepare Someone Else to Teach Children?

"All these things Jesus said to the crowds in parables; indeed, He said nothing to them without a parable." Matthew 13:34

I first titled this chapter "How Do I Prepare Someone Else to Teach a Lesson?" Then it dawned on me—Jesus didn't teach lessons; He taught *people*! We cannot prepare a lesson without thinking of the children who will sit before us. Yes, this chapter will be about preparing lesson plans, but they are a means to an end: sharing the Good News with children.

Before thinking about what your teachers need to know and do, let's first detour to some curriculum details. If you are satisfied with the current curriculum, you're ready to move on. If not, plan to do some homework and commit time to review, select, or edit. The steps remain the same whether the curriculum is used in Sunday School, Midweek, VBS, or another program altogether.

Determine those individuals with whom you need to collaborate. The pastor? Your planning team? The program staff? The board of education? It is important to have the appropriate decision-makers partner with you.

Once again, the place to begin is with the vision for your overall ministry as well as goals for the particular program whose curriculum is being scrutinized. For example, if you are selecting curriculum for your Midweek program, and your mission is to help the children learn how to serve others, the curriculum needs to share that same focus. If your VBS strives to reach neighborhood kids who don't know Jesus, the curriculum had better be Jesus-centered.

Here are some other questions that are important to ask. Is it . . .

» doctrinally sound?

» affordable?

» full of creative Bible teaching?

» age and developmentally appropriate?

» easily edited and adjusted to your program's format and timing?

» used without difficulty by volunteers with easily acquired supplies?

» filled with supplemental activities that connect to the lesson, such as music, games, and crafts?

» visually appealing, with colorful, up-to-date, multicultural take-home pieces that appeal to both sexes?

» thematically desirable, fun, memorable, and engaging for older kids?

The choice of curriculum is so important. Not only does it teach the children, but it also teaches the volunteers. I learned this the hard way many years ago when I thought I could use and edit a Sunday School curriculum with a Baptist bent. Because it held a different understanding of Baptism and faith creation, I constantly had to defend our denominational perspective to the staff while explaining the reasons behind the revisions. When we changed to a curriculum with a Lutheran viewpoint, it was more readily accepted and understood because the theology was already built in to the lessons.

However, the perfect curriculum (if there is such a thing!) is not a magic bullet that will make a program thrive. Programs succeed when God's faith-filled people use the lesson material as a tool to share truths about God and His Word with the children. And above all, it is the Holy Spirit who works faith and trust in hearts through the Word that children hear.

Don't assume that teachers know what to do with the curriculum they receive. Your responsibility is to train the staff to carry out your vision for how to creatively and effectively convey God's truths to the children. Consider modeling a lesson for the teachers before the session actually begins. If you demonstrate this lesson yourself, you will want to practice, practice, practice, or you may want to find a gifted teacher to instruct in your stead. It's much easier to develop good habits at the outset than to correct poor ones later on.

In order to set the stage before the program actually begins, gather your staff together. You'll need to be creative and offer several alternatives to increase the odds of their attending. Invite them to a meeting, sponsor a breakfast, share lunch after church, meet for coffee, host a dinner, or suggest dessert at your home. Over time, if you work hard at building relationships with your staff, they will become more eager to share their time with you.

Let's switch gears and get started on that lesson itself. If you are going to model a lesson to your staff in your first training session, you will also want to make use of these suggestions. Allow me to introduce you to the four Ps of lesson preparation—Pray, Plan, Practice, and Present. We will conclude with some comments about selecting and leading music.

PRAY

For what do we pray? For everything lesson-related! The place to begin is with oneself. Pray that the truths you teach the children will first take root in your own heart. I have taught lessons from my head, from my heart, and from obligation. I can tell the difference, and I'm sure the students can as well. When I teach a biblical truth to others that personally affects my own life, my teaching is more authentic and compelling. Dr. Howard Hendricks coined the law of the teacher: "If you stop growing today, you stop teaching tomorrow."

Pray that the Holy Spirit will give you one clear message for your lesson. Everything you do and teach should support this one main theme that must relate to the lives of the children. I've heard this referred to as total-session teaching, the truth, the theme, or the Bible point. Refuse the temptation to play a game or do a craft simply because it's fun—it needs to reinforce the truth that will be taught that day. It's terribly hard to discard a brilliant idea if it doesn't fit the theme, but you must ruthlessly set it aside. Ask the question, "What would I want kids to tell their parents when asked, 'What did you learn today?'" If you can articulate the answer, you have identified your main point.

Pray that the children are open to receive the message you plan to share. Only the Holy Spirit opens hearts, and we can claim the scriptural promise that God's Word will not return void.

PREPARE

Years ago, I frequently used a pressure cooker to prepare dinner for my family. It allowed me to wait until the last minute to put the meal together and still serve dinner on time. Now my go-to appliance is the Crock-Pot. The ingredients simmer for hours, and the meal is ready whenever hunger sets in.

Lesson preparation is best described as "Crock-Pot cooking." Allowing God's truths to slowly sink into our hearts and minds during the week is more life changing than last-minute preparations during the pressure-cooker time of Saturday night. On Sunday afternoon already, I like to look ahead at the next week's Bible readings and lesson theme so the truths can start to simmer and continue bubbling anytime, day or night.

Crock-Pot cooking allows time to meditate on the Scripture itself rather than merely reading the lesson from the curriculum. One of my morning devotional practices is meditating on the week's Scripture and asking God to open my eyes to how He wants to apply it in my own life. Being a learner always precedes being a teacher.

Even after all these years, one time-consuming aspect of my preparation is how to balance Law and Gospel. One would think it would be easier by now, but it is so easy to become moralistic: "Be brave like David when he fought Goliath." And yet ironically, if I hear another teacher say that, I want to scream, "I can't be brave on my own; I need God's help!" The source of power for life change is Christ in me. "He who began a good work in you will bring it to completion at the day of Jesus Christ" (Philippians 1:6). Bible characters are not heroes. They are as weak as you and I are. Think about Noah after leaving the ark or King David and his family life or the generational deceit in the lineage of Abraham, Isaac, and Jacob. God is the hero to whom we must always point. He accomplished what we could never accomplish on our own. The Law points out our sin and need for help, but the Good News of God's unconditional love in Christ is what offers us hope and the possibility of change. "God's kindness is meant to lead you to repentance" (Romans 2:4).

Spreading out lesson planning throughout the week also allows time to consider whether all the suggested activities are practical and developmentally appropriate. I recall a lesson during the winter that suggested playing indoor water games. Call me a spoilsport, but I wasn't up to dealing with wet kids on a cold Sunday morning. A hot summer day of VBS? Of course!

Plan how you will use the Bible in your lesson. Whether you simply show the Bible and ask young kids to repeat the ditty "The Bible is true, true, true" or whether you ask a question and have older students read verses to find the answer, God's tangible Word must be an integral part of each lesson.

As you think through the lesson schedule, mentally picture the layout of your room. Imagine where the children will go and what they will do when they first arrive. How and by whom will they be greeted? How will transitions be handled? You probably won't want to begin a time of prayer right after a high-energy game! How will the children be safely dismissed to their parents? Think through these details during the week to pave the way for a smoother class time together.

Allow time to gather the proper materials. Few kids wait quietly and patiently in their seats with their hands to themselves while the teacher hunts down glue sticks or yarn. Think about the roles your helpers will play, and prepare to share your expectations of what they will do during class. And of course, you will want to arrive early to get your room or space ready to receive the children. As the adage goes, "Class begins when the first learner arrives."

PRACTICE

Don't take anything for granted, especially if you are a new teacher, so be sure to practice each portion of the lesson. Make the craft, lead the game, teach the songs, and rehearse the Bible story. When class time arrives, you'll walk into the room feeling much more confident and prepared.

There are so many creative ways to present Bible stories. Your curriculum is probably already filled with suggestions. In case you're starting from scratch, as the cooks in my family say, here is a list of ideas to get you started.

» Actions—As you tell the Bible story, act it out or have the kids panto-mime motions.

» Voices—Have the kids count the days of creation or make animal sounds when the ark is loaded up.

» Hats—Put on a different hat for each Bible character in the Bible story.

» Chalk art/whiteboard drawing/mural—Draw simple sketches while telling the story or listening to an audio recording.

» Flip chart—Make simple sketches ahead of time on a flip chart, and show the pictures while telling the story.

» Scroll—Draw simple sketches on a scroll; unroll it as you tell the story.

» Rubbing—Put flat items or cardstock cutouts under a blank sheet of paper that is taped to the wall. Rub a peeled crayon over the items while telling the story.

» Torn or cut paper—As you tell the story, tear or cut the paper into appropriate shapes.

» Puzzles—Cut posters of the story into puzzle pieces ahead of time and put them together while speaking.

» Sand table—Gather the children around the sand table and use figures in the sand to tell the story.

» Story bag or treasure box—Collect visuals and put them in a bag or treasure box. Take them out one at a time as you speak.

» Visual aids—Show pictures, posters, flannelgraphs, or maps.

» Figurines/dolls/three-dimensional objects—Use these as story props.

» Books—Read or show pictures from a pop-up or Bible story book.

» Skits—Assign parts to kids in a readers theater.

» Drama—Invite a drama team to put on a play for your class.

» Costume—Act out the story from a first-person perspective.

» Costumes/accessories—Change costumes or accessories as you act.

» Interview—Question an eyewitness who "saw" the Bible event occur.

» Video/DVD—Plan to use only use short segments. Tell the children the main idea and give them something to look for in the movie. Pause it occasionally for discussion.

» Puppet team—Invite a team to present the story.

» Individual puppet—Use any variety of puppet (sock puppet, paper bag puppet, stuffed animal, faces drawn on sticks, plastic spoon puppets, wooden spoon puppets, finger puppets, etc.) to tell a story or engage in a conversation.

» Whispering puppet—Speak to the puppet who responds in a whisper only to the teacher, who then relays the message to the children.

» Online video clip—Use to introduce the day's theme for older kids.

Teach your lesson to an imaginary class, to the mirror, or to a friend, spouse, or child. The more comfortable you feel, the more you will be able to focus on the children rather than on your notes. Make easy-to-read notes if they will be helpful. During your own days as a student, you probably heard monotone readings from the curriculum; don't be that kind of lackluster teacher yourself! Practice eye contact. Children (and adults) are more connected when you look at them. Practicing helps work out the kinks that you didn't know were there until you actually tried implementing the lesson. Anticipate things that may be problematic so you can come prepared with solutions.

PRESENT

The day has arrived, and it's finally time to present the lesson from a heart that has been prepared by God. We all know that at times, the best we can give is what we put together at the last minute. God understands time crunches. But don't allow this to become a habit; you and your children will be short-changed of the blessings that come from exploring deeply all He has done for you.

Whether you are preparing a Sunday School lesson, a children's message for the worship service, or a talk to parents, the process is the same. That Crock-Pot serves up tasty meals in all these settings.

SELECTING AND LEADING MUSIC

The four Ps of lesson preparation also apply to the process of selecting and leading music for groups of children or families: Pray, Prepare, Practice, and Present.

A friend named Jenny recently spent time with my Concordia students to give them some instruction and experience leading music. She said that our words, facial expressions, and body language can all be used either to communicate the greatness of our God or to point to ourselves. We prayerfully chose the former.

Jenny encouraged the students to look carefully at the words of a song to identify its primary objective. Are the words directed *to* God, encouraging the children to worship Him? If so, use this time to worship God yourself. You may want to demonstrate a worshipful posture such as closing your eyes or looking upward so the children can learn from your example. Do the words tell truths or stories *about* God? If so, make eye contact with the children as if you are telling them about His wonders. Rejoice in your own heart about the works of God in your life. Are the words just silly and fun to get the kids moving? (Think of the classic "Father Abraham.") Then have fun and be silly yourself!

If you are in a position to select the music, you will naturally look for songs that are appropriate for the age and understanding of the children and that have words consistent with our spiritual heritage.

You will want to present each song with a verbal introduction. Be brief! If you are able, tie it into the Bible story or truth for the day's lesson.

Here are a few more nuggets from Jenny:

» If using a CD, make sure the player is working and the CD is compatible.

» Teaching a brand-new song requires breaking it down into its parts for several weeks in a row.

>> Find a repeating phrase or chorus with which to begin. Say those words and do the motions, asking the kids to repeat them after you. You may want to focus only on the chorus for the first week.

» When an instrumental break comes in the music, you can say the next phrase the kids will be singing to refresh their memories and get them started on the next verse.

» If you can't carry a tune and still need to lead the music, you can say the words while the music is playing.

» If leading a set of two to three songs, introduce the newer song first or second. Then end on a confident note with a song the children know and love.

* * * *

My most memorable lessons are those led by my second- and third-grade students. Each year upon establishing relationships and routines, I ask students if they would like to lead a five-to-ten-minute teaching time in a future week. One in particular from last year left me speechless. Young Gunnar led a lesson on building your house on sand or rock. He read from the Bible then led us to a poster he had drawn, displaying the differences. As questions were asked, Gunnar pointed out that the man who had built his house on the sand was asleep and "had no idea what was going on." This was not something he had planned to focus on, but it led to such a deep discussion and left us all greatly moved. The Holy Spirit was moving that night through our young teacher.

Carol Zachrich
Woodside Bible Church
Romeo, MI

* * * *

Mini Articles for Teachers

THE 4 Ps OF LESSON PREPARATION

What a beautiful opportunity to allow the Holy Spirit to grow your own faith as you teach His Word to children. Using the four Ps will seal His Word in your own heart.

1. Pray

- Pray for yourself, that God's Word first takes root in your own heart and that you can share the message with conviction and joy.
- Pray for your students, that they are open to hearing the message.

2. Prepare

- Read the Scriptures and the lesson theme early in the week, and think about it as you move throughout your days.
- Consider your students' attributes and decide whether the suggested activities are appropriate.
- Clarify how each activity can support the day's theme.
- Consider how you will use the Bible during your lesson time.
- Think about how you will transition from one activity to another.
- Gather your needed materials.
- Consider how your helpers can best assist.
- Plan to arrive at your room early to set up.

3. Practice

- Practice, practice, practice until you can teach the Bible lesson with maximum eye contact.
- Practice leading the craft or game to make sure each step feels effortless.

4. Present

- Present with joy—you are ready!

TOTAL-SESSION TEACHING

So much to teach and so little time! Teachers who experience this tension are tempted to use one setting to instruct kids about creation, Solomon's wisdom, and Jesus' ascension all at the same time. This is an exaggeration, of course, but the truth is that narrowing down our lesson to focus on one clear message is hard work.

This focal point is referred to as the truth, the theme, or the Bible point, and using this approach is called total-session teaching.

Everything you do and teach should support this one main theme. Refuse the temptation to play a game or do a craft simply because it's fun—it needs to reinforce the truth that will be taught that day. It's terribly hard to discard a brilliant idea if it doesn't fit the theme, but you must ruthlessly set it aside.

Have you heard parents ask their kids, "What did you learn today?" What would you want your students to answer? If you can articulate a clear reply, you have identified your main point. And do make sure that this main point relates to the lives of the children.

Here are some examples:

» Faith is trusting what God says more than what my eyes can see.

» When bad things happen, God is always near to help us.

» Jesus is our treasure.

BALANCING LAW AND GOSPEL

The SOS acronym is simple. The Law "Shows Our Sin" and the Gospel "Shows Our Savior." But using both in our teaching in ways that are faithful to how God works is not so simple. Here's why.

We want to see kids' lives change and reflect Christ. We want to know that what we're teaching is making a difference. We naturally slip into becoming moralistic: "Be brave like David when he fought Goliath." "Keep your eyes on Jesus so you don't sink like Peter."

But the truth of the matter is that we can't be brave on our own. We can't keep our eyes on Jesus all the time, despite knowing the importance. We desperately need God's help! These statements are the voice of the Law. The Law shows us our inability to live up to God's desires for us. The Law in itself cannot empower change in our hearts or our behavior.

The source of power for life change is Christ in me. "He who began a good work in you will bring it to completion at the day of Jesus Christ" (Philippians 1:6). This is the Gospel, the good news of hope.

The people in the Bible story are *not* the heroes. Think about King David and his moral failures or Peter and his runaway mouth. These men are as weak as you and I are.

God is the hero to whom we must always point. He accomplished what we could never accomplish on our own. The Law points out our sin and need for help, but the Gospel of God's unconditional love in Christ is what offers us hope and the possibility of change. "God's kindness is meant to lead you to repentance" (Romans 2:4).

Kids desperately need to hear the Gospel. Be the one to share this message of hope.

THE 4 Ps OF LEADING MUSIC

Have you caught yourself humming a tune midday or repeating lyrics in your mind in the middle of the night? Music is a powerful tool to settle God's Word deeply into the hearts of kids.

1. Pray

Pray that our words, facial expressions, and body language communicate the greatness of our God rather than point to ourselves. Pray that the children experience the joy of freely praising God.

2. Prepare

Look carefully at the words of a song to identify its primary objective. If the words are directed to God, feel free to use this time to worship God yourself as you lead the children. You may want to demonstrate a worshipful posture, such as closing your eyes or looking upward, so the children can learn from your example. If the words tell truths or stories about God, you can rejoice in your own heart about the works of God in your life. Make eye contact with the children as if you are telling them about His wonders. If the words are just silly and fun, have fun and be silly yourself as you get the kids moving.

Be sure to select music that is appropriate to the age and understanding of the children and that has words consistent with our spiritual heritage. If you will be leading a set of two to three songs, introduce the newer song first or second. Then end on a positive note with a song the kids all know and love.

3. Practice

Think about a way to present each song with a verbal introduction. Be brief. If you are able, tie it into the Bible story or truth for the day's lesson.

If you use a CD, be sure to practice with the actual disc and player you'll use to make sure it works and the CD is compatible.

Teaching a brand-new song requires breaking it down into its parts for several weeks in a row.

Find a repeating phrase or chorus with which to begin. Say those words and do the motions, asking the kids to repeat them after you; then sing them together. You may want to focus only on the chorus for the first week.

When an instrumental break comes in the music, you can say the next phrase the kids will be singing to refresh their memories and get them started on the next verse.

If you are one of the unfortunate ones who can't carry a tune and still needs to lead the music, you can say the words while the music is playing.

4. Present

You're on!

HOW TO TEACH A CHILD TO PRAY ALOUD

Here are some ideas to help your children learn to talk to God about the everyday things in their lives. Some of the suggestions serve as first steps and merely allow the children to hear their own voices; others can be used as they become more comfortable with impromptu prayer.

1. Model oral prayer yourself using short, conversational words.

2. Ask the children to repeat the phrases you speak—"Thank You,

God . . . *Thank You, God* . . . for sending Your Son . . . *for sending Your Son . . ."*

3. Pray the Lord's Prayer or another prayer aloud together.

4. Make various statements about God ("You love us so much . . . You forgive all our sins . . . ") and ask the children to respond as a group after each statement with a phrase like "We praise You, God" or "We love You, God."

5. Make a statement and ask the children to respond aloud with any thoughts that fit the category—"God, we thank You for things that we can hear . . ." (children respond with things like birds, music, Dad's voice, etc.). Or the teacher may say, "We ask You, God, to help these people . . ." (children respond, "Mom," "Grandma," etc.).

6. Do a waterfall prayer, with all praying aloud at the same time.

7. Ask the children to think about what the Bible tells us about Jesus. Say, "Let's tell Jesus how He makes us happy." Children respond aloud.

8. Use prayer cards. Before class, write "I praise You because . . .," "Thank You for . . .," and "Please help me . . ." on cards. Ask children to take a card and complete the sentence aloud.

9. Ask a child to pray one sentence—"Susie, will you ask God to help Billy feel better?"

10. Ask a child to write a prayer at home and read it to the class next week.

11. Ask a child to thank God for the food before snack time.

12. Be very quiet. Ask the children to think of questions they would like to ask God and to say them out loud.

13. Make a prayer wall. Each child removes another person's written prayer request posted on the wall and prays about it aloud.

During prayer time, vary your posture: fold hands, hold hands open, hold hands up to God, hold hands in a circle, gather in a football huddle, or kneel.

Curriculum Selection Guidelines

Is the curriculum you are considering . . .

» compatible with your purpose, vision, mission, and values?

» doctrinally sound?

» affordable?

» compatible with your time frame and program calendar?

» in harmony with the program format that works best for your church?

» creative, with creative Bible presentations and more activities than just worksheets?

» age and developmentally appropriate?

» edited easily?

» easily usable by volunteers and the director or superintendent?

» filled with supplemental activities like catchy music, fun and noncompetitive games, and creative crafts using supplies that can be easily acquired?

» visually appealing, with colorful, up-to-date, multicultural take-home pieces that appeal to both sexes?

» thematically desirable (especially for VBS)?

» memorable, captivating, fun, and appealing to older kids (especially the boys)?

Is Communication Really That Critical?

"Oh give thanks to the LORD; call upon His name; make known His deeds among the peoples!" Psalm 105:1

The short answer to the question posed by the chapter title is a resounding yes! People need information and, when caught off guard, usually don't take too well to being left out of the loop. A few weeks ago, our neighborhood read in the local paper about a new condo complex to be built at the end of our street. Hearing about the building project in such an impersonal and roundabout way brought unhappy neighbors to city meetings ready to speak their minds.

Communication is critical. The word embodies the broad scope of conveying information and receiving feedback, whether it is oral or written, private or public. Because trust is built when people are well informed, communication must be proactive and never assumed. On the other hand, a lack of communication breeds uncertainty and confusion at best and can lead to misinformation, suspicion, and even conflict.

Communication involves relaying information about the past, the present, and the future. People want to hear stories about prior events, about what is currently going on, and about what is going to take place in the future. Therefore, it's important to simultaneously think of all three time frames—past, present, and future—as you relay needed information to the appropriate people groups.

Publicity is part of the overall communication process. It is generally the more specific act of disseminating and promoting news about a particular event. For example, informing third-grade parents about the upcoming classes when their children will receive Bibles requires publicity so that people can attend. People can't come to events, activities, or opportunities that they don't even know exist.

Some church leaders find the word *publicity* more palatable than *advertising* or *marketing*, which can conjure up images of the business world. But language aside, it's critical for all leaders to scrutinize their intended audiences and ask how best to convey necessary information. Regardless what word is used, the task at hand is to study "customers" and let them know what is happening and how their needs will be addressed.

Promotion requires a financial investment, whether that means purchasing higher-quality paper and colored ink for a special brochure or placing an ad in the local newspaper for a one-time event targeting the community. Funds may be needed to hire someone to create an attractive flyer with graphics that will pique interest. The objective is for people to take a second look at a handout or brochure rather than immediately toss it into the recycling bin.

Even if you are on a strict budget, there are ways to capture attention and avoid the *b* word: *boring*. Whether you're speaking or writing or preparing literature, boring is not allowed, unless you're advertising for a snail race—and even that could be turned into fun with a little creativity! "Move Up with the Big Kids" sounds more appealing than "Sunday School starts again next week." Would you rather go to "Games, Good Food, and Goodies Galore!" or the "Sunday School Picnic"?

It's important to get right to the point and be concise, not wordy. This holds true for all communication, both oral and written. For example, perhaps you decide to invest in a phone blitz. Think about the split-second decision you personally make to either hang up the phone or listen to a prerecorded advertisement. "St. Paul's VBS starts on Monday and we hope to see you and your friends at 10:00 a.m." may keep more people listening than adding nonessentials like "Hello, how are you? I'm volunteering at St. Paul Lutheran Church and am calling all the parents to remind you about VBS, which starts next Monday at 10:00 a.m. Our theme is *Barnyard Roundup*. Would your kids want to invite any friends to come with them?"

One basic publicity piece that could enhance your congregation's communication efforts is a generic children's ministry brochure. Having a brochure serves two purposes. First, it presses you as the leader to examine and assess all the ways your church serves children and their families. It allows you to review your V/P/M, goals, and values and determine whether yours is a "good product" to share, one that exudes quality and evokes enthusiasm. Second, it gives you an informational tool to offer people within your congregation as well as guests and those not yet connected. Once it's created, you will find countless ways to use and distribute this brochure.

Creating a brochure is greatly simplified with the templates available in programs such as Microsoft Publisher. Choose child-friendly graphics and colors, and use language that is welcoming and easily understood. Put yourself in the shoes of someone unfamiliar with your ministry, and consider what that person would want or need to know.

Once your draft is complete, try to read it as if you knew nothing about your current ministry. Note any key information that may be missing. You may even want to ask someone with an outside perspective to read your text for clarity. This advice holds true for any communication effort. Sometimes we are too close to an event or idea to be objective.

There are so many ways to relay information.

- » Church website
- » Bulletin
- » Newsletter
- » TV monitors at church
- » Social media
- » Email
- » Postcards or letters

» Flyers

» Text messages

» Invitations for church members to give friends

» Announcements or testimonies in church services

» Videos or skits in church services

» Announcements in meetings and Bible studies

» Preprinted stickers on young children

» Exterior signage

» Door-to-door flyers

» Bulletin boards at church

» Community bulletin boards

» Local newspaper articles

» Local newspaper community calendar

» Phone blitz

» A previous event to publicize the next one

» People to tell their friends

» One-on-one conversations

» Banner-carrying plane (just checking to see if you're still reading!)

In a church setting, a number of individuals and people groups need to be kept informed. This requires looking through a lens other than your own. The level of detail and kinds of information will vary from group to group, but all need to know what's taking place in your mind and on the calendar. And they will need different types of information before, during, and after the event itself.

Let's get practical and look at a number of people groups and imagine what each would need to know about VBS.

PASTOR/BOARDS

Pastors and boards do not like to be surprised about anything taking place in their church that they know nothing about. As early as you can, give them the major details about your upcoming VBS—the date, time, theme, description of activities, what you'll do differently this year, the target audience, and what you hope to accomplish. Because children's ministry is part of the entire ministry of the church, point out how VBS will support the church's overall mission.

As time goes on, keep them informed about the planning process. They won't want to hear every tiny detail, but they will want to know if you are on target or if major glitches take place along the way. If appropriate, give updates during the VBS week itself. Invite them to come to an assembly or evening program in order to physically see what is taking place. Giving them a role to play, such as greeting parents or leading the prayer, may encourage them to more readily accept your invitation.

When VBS is over and you have a moment to catch your breath, give these leaders a verbal or written report. How many children attended? How did this year compare to previous ones? What stories can you share about volunteers, parents, or kids? How did VBS meet the intended purpose? What might you tweak for next summer?

Trust is built when you are open and take the initiative to keep people informed. You will need the endorsement of the pastor and the leadership boards to promote your vision and your ideas, so keep communicating! Give them copies of parent newsletters and include them on the family email list. Make presentations at staff or board meetings. Challenge them to consider what your church would be like without a children's ministry. Pastors and boards can only support what they know.

STAFF

In some settings, "staff" means a group of paid individuals. If you work in a locale with a paid team, all will benefit by the momentum that is created when more ministries get on the same page. Imagine partnering with your church's women's ministry to inform the MOPS group about VBS or connecting with the senior ministry to ask for volunteers to babysit Sunday School teachers' little ones who are too young to attend. Consider the benefit of teaming up with teens to give flyers to families on their outing to the trampoline park.

Or "staff" may mean the secretary and custodian who keep the church running and support the pastor. Can you imagine cleaning up all your own VBS messes each day? I didn't think so! Or running off all those flyers or evening programs yourself? Hardly! Informing them of your needs early gives them the time to prepare for this more intense season of ministry. Expressing your appreciation lifts up people who can easily be taken for granted. Holding out your vision for reaching more kids with the Good News of Jesus helps custodians and secretaries find a deeper purpose behind the critical but tedious tasks they complete for you and for the rest of the congregation.

Or "staff" may mean the volunteers who offer their time, talents, and treasures to serve God in all the ways VBS requires. Volunteers are the backbone of VBS and not only need but also deserve clearly communicated information.

CONGREGATION

Those of us serving in children's ministry can easily get caught up in our own corner of the church with our own teams and forget that we are part of a greater whole, the congregation itself. A congregation has the potential to support and bless its children's ministry with prayer, finances, volunteers, and encouragement. Wouldn't it be amazing if your VBS could be buoyed by these endeavors? To make this dream a reality, the congregation needs to know what took place in previous years, what's happening this summer, and what your hopes are for the future. Use every means possible to tell the stories of what is taking place in your program and why.

One exception to my "communicate, communicate, communicate" mantra relates to recruitment. The congregation is indeed the source for volunteer personnel, but please do not incessantly publicize your need for more helpers. Desperation does not incite enthusiasm. It may provoke guilt, but guilty volunteers rarely experience the joy of serving with their gifts. It is appropriate to communicate your needs, but please do so carefully and rarely. Publicize the event or program before expressing your volunteer needs.

Consider consolidating your requests for help into one or two recruitment campaigns per year. For example, in the spring, you might want to ask for summer VBS volunteers at the same time you ask for fall Sunday School teachers. You could develop a catchy theme such "20/20 Vision—

20 volunteers in 20 days" or use puzzle graphics to promote "Which Piece Are You?" If the congregation senses that something exciting is taking place in your ministry, they will be more likely to want to be part of it.

In addition to the previously given list of ways to relay information, here are a few more means of highlighting children's ministry to the entire congregation:

» Interview a child or family so they can share their faith story.

» Show a purchased video about children's ministry.

» Create your own video about children or their families.

» Highlight volunteers in the worship service—honor their longevity or pray for them when a program begins.

» Ask your pastor to talk about the church's vision for children and families in his sermon.

» Share kids' talents—ask them to sing or play their instruments during worship.

» Have a children's art fair based on an upcoming worship service theme.

» Host a ministry fair where each ministry can inform the congregation of their activities.

TEAM

For a number of years, I had been beating the drum for improved communication in our church. So when a co-worker criticized me for withholding necessary information from our team, I was taken aback. Upon further reflection, I realized she was right. Being an introvert, I usually work toward a decision internally and privately. The members of my immediate team were not privy to my inner ruminations, and I had failed to keep them sufficiently informed of the process. They deserved—and received—an apology.

Your ministry team is the group closest to you, so please be mindful that they, too, need to hear what is taking place in your heart each step of the way. Let them know what VBS curricula you are considering long before the decision must be made. Get their input about how to improve the closing program. Invite them to help you process the end results after the last crayons are put away.

VOLUNTEERS

In earlier chapters, we spoke of the need for volunteers to be informed of safety protocols and job descriptions so they can complete their tasks. Part of this vital information is the time commitment they will be asked to make. Provide a variety of options so they are able to serve within their means.

Volunteers also need to know the big picture of what's happening in other areas of children's ministry. This enables sports coaches to promote VBS and empowers VBS teachers to tell parents about Sunday School or the annual fall party. They will gain a perspective of the ministry that is broader than their own specific area of service. They will glimpse a greater vision of the work in which they have been given a privileged part.

Serving in ministry is never meant to be a solo endeavor. As the Body of Christ, we all contribute to God's mission of building the Kingdom. It takes deliberate effort to remain connected to your volunteers, effort that is not only worthwhile but also critical.

PARENTS

Between school, sports, music lessons, church activities, and occasional visits to see Grandma and Grandpa, kids and families have busy lives. Parents need to know what's happening well in advance. Work hard to be one step ahead of the calendar. For example, distribute your VBS brochures well in advance at the Easter fair. Use your VBS newsletter to promote the fall harvest party.

Because there are so many options from which to choose, parents need to know the benefits their children will experience as a result of your program. They may not care that their children will hear a particular Bible story, but they will care that their children have fun in a safe environment with good, moral teaching. Keep this in mind when you create your promotional materials.

Parents can be your best promoters. If their children want to come to your events, they will be the first to tell other parents about the fun and worthwhile activities at your church. So be sure to offer programs with excellence and give them all the information they need to share the details with their friends. Flyers, handouts, brochures, emails, and texts can easily be passed along to others in their friendship and neighborhood circles.

One question on our VBS enrollment form this year asked, "How did you hear about VBS?" The most frequent response? Friends!

KIDS

Have you taken note of the questions parents ask their kids when picking them up after class or an activity? Maybe you ask these questions of your own children. Question 1: "Did you have fun?" Question 2: "What did you learn?"

If you want kids to come to a church activity, they need to know that it will be fun. Learning about Jesus and growing a relationship with Him takes precedence in your mind, but it must include a fun factor from the kids' perspective. Be sure to let kids and parents know about all the fun activities when you are telling them about VBS. *Boring* is a four-letter word to kids!

Look at VBS through the eyes of the children who will potentially attend to gain clues about what your publicity efforts should highlight. Children want to know: Will I know where to go and what to do? Will I have fun? Will I be alone? Will I have fun? Will I make friends? Will I have fun? Will my mom find me? Will I have fun? A bit redundant, but you get the idea.

NEIGHBORHOOD AND COMMUNITY

"What if your church didn't exist anymore? Would it make any difference to the neighborhood around your church?" I don't recall where I first heard this question, but it affects me to this day. It also provides the motivation to let neighbors know what we are about and how we can serve them.

No longer do we live in an era when people take the initiative to seek out the church. In fact, the church and churchgoers are often seen as a place and people to avoid. Oh, there are exceptions of course. But the initiative to invite lies with us. Do it!

Our church is beginning to reach into our neighborhood in small ways. Last Christmas, we went Christmas caroling and passed out candy canes with a Christmas blessing for each home. This summer, we hosted an outdoor movie night featuring family-friendly activities and a G-rated movie for kids. Each goodie bag had candy and a kazoo, along with a children's ministry brochure and movie discussion questions with a spiritual application.

VBS is a perfect opportunity to invite neighborhood kids. After all, parents won't have to go far to bring their kids. Summer is the time tired moms seek cost-effective and fun activities to occupy their children. Make the most of it!

You will undoubtedly find even more opportunities to communicate than those listed here. That's great! Don't hesitate to set aside plenty of time in your working schedule to develop a publicity strategy. In fact, this task is one of the most critical on your to-do list as a ministry leader. That's why an entire chapter is devoted to the subject.

With information available today at the touch of a screen, people who are "church shopping" will rely on your church's website to gain information about your identity and ministry. If you haven't already done so, Google the names of several churches in your area. It won't take long for you to get a sense of the kinds of people they hope to attract (or not!). Finding information for events long passed may hint at the need for technical assistance, or it may reveal a lack of urgency to connect with the community. What image does your church promote via its website?

A final note—don't forget to consider your motivation when creating communication plans. Jesus challenges us to look deeply and discern the motivations in our hearts. One way I test motivation is to ask who I want to glorify through my promotional efforts—myself and my image or God alone? When I find myself wanting people to voice what a great job we're doing, I know it's time to enter the prayer closet to repent, to rest in God's affirmation, and to ask Him for a greater desire to bring glory to Him alone.

* * * *

Building a healthy team is very important to me as a children's ministry director. I place a high value on communication. Each week I spend time one on one with the children's ministry staff, and we meet twice a month as a team. During our meetings, I ask each person to share what is happening in his or her department. The updates are to help each person value what the others are doing in ministry, to pray for one another and learn from each other. The time together also helps to break down silos in ministry.

Sarah Arndt
Children's Ministry Director
Faith Lutheran Church
Troy, MI

* * * *

FaithKids Preschool has a Facebook page. I use it to remind parents about upcoming events and show them interesting things that are happening in the classrooms. Although we have a media release form on file for each child, we are careful not to put a child's face on Facebook. Not all parents are comfortable with their child's picture being on a public page on social media, and we respect that. The benefits of having a Facebook page are being able to share what is happening in preschool and receiving free publicity. The challenge is being able to do so without using pictures that identify our students.

Kerri Elliott
FaithKids Preschool Director
Faith Lutheran Church
Troy, MI

* * * *

We use Facebook and email for connecting with families and parents. We explored Twitter and Instagram, but have no one to keep them up properly. We have a website that we would like to put more family resources on, with links and recommendations.

Pastor Bill Wangelin
Our Savior Lutheran Church
Lansing, MI

* * * *

Q: Which social media tools do you use and how? What are the pros and cons?

A: Facebook and Instagram—The pros would be connecting with families, having a communication tool, and advertising our church events. The cons would be that there are a lot of negative posts on social media that can influence people in the wrong way and that when people pick and choose what to look at, they don't always read your positive post among all the noise of social media.

Eric Steinke
DCE
St. John's Lutheran Church
Adrian, MI

* * * *

Q: Which social media tools do you use and how? What are the pros and cons?

A: Church/school website, Facebook, Instagram, Twitter. Pros: It keeps me connected and can be a good communication tool. Cons: It can be a time waster if you're not disciplined.

Julie Burgess
Director of Family Life
St. Paul Lutheran Church and School
Ann Arbor, MI

* * * *

10 Steps to Create a Children's Ministry Brochure

1. Write rough draft summaries on the following topics:

   a. Purpose/mission/vision/values/goals

   b. Your primary disciple-making effort or program, such as a church-wide home Bible reading endeavor or Sunday School

   c. Worship service schedule and what is offered for children, such as children's bulletins, children's message, activity bags, etc.

   d. Additional ongoing classes or opportunities for children, parents, or families, such as Sunday School, Midweek classes, or parenting classes

   e. One-time classes or opportunities for children, parents, or families, such as VBS or a milestone event

   f. Preschool or Day School information

   g. Statement about training and screening your volunteers

2. Read and edit these summaries so people not connected with your ministry would find answers to their questions.

3. Include contact information for the ministry as a whole or for individual classes or events mentioned above.

4. Locate an attractive, child-friendly template on Microsoft Publisher (or another program), and insert your information.

5. Add graphics and adjust colors as needed.

6. Ask several people to read and edit the brochure.

7. Finalize the suggested edits.

8. List the ways you will use the brochure within the congregation.

9. List the ways you will use the brochure outside of the congregation.

10. Use it!

Communication Checklist

To explore all the possibilities for communicating an upcoming event, try the following exercise. Jot down what needs to be conveyed to the following people/groups before an event or program takes place. Then note what means you will use and the dates that serve as your deadlines.

Event:_____

Event Date:_____

People Group	Before	During	After
Pastor/Boards SAMPLE	What: *Inform about dates and theme for VBS* How: *Verbally at meeting* When: *1/12 Board Meeting*	What: *Report that 10 more unchurched children are attending this year* How: *Email* When: *7/18*	What: *Tell them about follow-up plan for these new families* How: *PowerPoint at meeting* When: *8/2 Board Meeting*
Pastor/Boards	What: How: When:	What: How: When:	What: How: When:
Staff	What: How: When:	What: How: When:	What: How: When:

Congregation	What:	What:	What:
	How:	How:	How:
	When:	When:	When:
Team	What:	What:	What:
	How:	How:	How:
	When:	When:	When:
Volunteers	What:	What:	What:
	How:	How:	How:
	When:	When:	When:
Parents	What:	What:	What:
	How:	How:	How:
	When:	When:	When:
Kids	What:	What:	What:
	How:	How:	How:
	When:	When:	When:
Neighborhood	What:	What:	What:
	How:	How:	How:
	When:	When:	When:

Pros and Cons of Social Networking as a Communication Tool for Churches

Pros

- » Can increase interactions with people
- » Disseminates information quickly
- » Enhances the number of contacts through networking
- » Low-cost means of publicizing events
- » Opportunity to influence people's thinking
- » Can increase traffic to church website
- » Can gather opinions quickly
- » Connects people with similar interests
- » Easily share photos

Cons

- » Time-consuming
- » Can spread hurtful or false information
- » Lessens face-to-face interaction
- » Can invite negative feedback
- » Requires daily monitoring and updates
- » Challenges privacy

Chapter 12

Leading, Following, or Both?

> "If I then, your Lord and Teacher, have washed your feet, you
> also ought to wash one another's feet. For I have given you an
> example, that you also should do just as I have done to you.
> Truly, truly, I say to you, a servant is not greater than his mas-
> ter, nor is a messenger greater than the one who sent him."
> John 13:14–16

The phrase "servant leadership" was newly coined by Robert Greenleaf in the corporate setting when I first heard it used by my professors at Concordia Teacher's College in Seward. The originator criticized domineering leaders and raised the values of serving, listening, and respect. He wanted to counteract the drive for power and the thirst to accumulate wealth and possessions. Because these values reflect Jesus' life and bring to mind the image of His washing His disciples' feet, the phrase caught on in Christian circles.

Servant leadership obviously involves serving people. That is a key part of our call as Christ-followers. But can you imagine trying to serve each and every individual who expresses a need? That task would be exhausting at best and is hardly what God intended for His people. I believe that servant leadership should actually entail serving God first. This was Jesus' primary goal—His obedient relationship with His Father created the deep pool of reserve

171

that secondarily empowered Him to serve others. Listening to God first set the agenda for how and where He met the needs of people.

Imagine a parent whose primary goal is to serve his or her child. On the surface, this sounds like a worthy endeavor, but if there is no deeper underpinning of wanting the son or daughter to have a heart for others, the child will predictably grow into a narcissistic individual who thinks the world owes him or her everything. Likewise, if we try to serve people foremost, there may be some undesirable results because a deeper objective—God!—is lacking. Putting others before God will tempt us to say yes to everything, even those things that may not be in our or God's best interest. It may not even serve the best interests of those who seek something from you—their real need might be to learn patience or humility, for example. Serving people first elevates the created to the position that only the Creator deserves.

During Jesus' tenure on earth, He perfectly demonstrated dependence on His—and our—heavenly Father. One clear picture of their relationship emerges at His Baptism. "This is My beloved Son, with whom I am well pleased" (Matthew 3:17). His Father's words of affirmation initiate Jesus' call to ministry. Jesus' identity as God's beloved Son enabled Him to face temptation in obedience to the Father's will and to endure humility for our sake (Philippians 2:8). In Christ, our summons as God's children enables us to trust our heavenly Father as we face the struggles in our own lives.

Discipleship is all about being connected to the vine as our source of strength. That place of communion with God is the deep well from which leadership emerges. During one of the Catalyst conferences entitled "Courage," Britt Merrick advised, "Stop trying to be a leader for God and start being a lover of God." Following Jesus takes much higher precedence—and more time—than following advice from the latest leadership book.

If God has called you to lead people as part of your faith journey, you may find yourself identifying with Moses, Gideon, and Jeremiah—men who thought their weaknesses defined them. I love the image of God's naming Gideon "mighty warrior" while he was still hiding out in a winepress. God saw something within him that he could not see himself, something that God Himself would provide. God's long-distance vision was quite unlike his and ours. If you have a natural inclination toward leadership, praise God! If you find yourself kicking and screaming at the call like the individuals previously mentioned, praise Him as well! He promises to provide all you need to carry out the mission of making a difference in the lives of children and families in the Church and in the world.

Because God has given us different personalities, aptitudes, and gifts, has schooled us through different circumstances, and has called us to serve in different settings, how can we ever conclude that leadership has one expression? Brazen Peter, reassuring Barnabas, helpful Dorcas—each of their paths of following Jesus and leading others to Him looked different. And yet in our own lives, we look at prominent Christian leaders today and wonder why we don't measure up to them. There's no one right way to lead. In fact, both the realms of business and church have attempted to identify different leadership styles. My purpose is not to offer my own inventory, but rather to remind us that our creative God knows what He is doing in shaping us to carry out His work in unique and various ways. Don't envy what He has placed in another.

We each possess weaknesses and strengths, and God uses both to accomplish His purposes. Weaknesses keep us dependent on Him. Strengths allow us to make unique contributions in His service.

Given some thought, you may agree with the authors of the Strengths-Finder assessment that people are more effective when they employ their strengths rather than try to improve their weaknesses.[15] My team and I found taking the StrengthsFinder inventory to be a very affirming exercise that helped identify our primary areas of giftedness. This exercise helped us better understand and appreciate one another. We experienced firsthand that fully using our strengths filled us with joy because we were serving in ways compatible with how God created us.

Two years ago, students from the Concordia Universities in Ann Arbor and Austin visited King of Kings Lutheran Church in Omaha. We observed their staff wearing shirts with their personal primary strengths embroidered on the sleeves. This attire was a tangible attempt to honor each person as God's unique creation.

---

15 Tom Rath, *StrengthsFinder 2.0* (New York: Gallup Press, 2007).

360-DEGREE LEADERSHIP

In the year 2000, I attended the Leadership Summit at Willow Creek Community Church. One of Bill Hybels's presentations was entitled "The 360-Degree Leader." I took notes like crazy and still earmark this talk as one of his classic and timeless presentations. The word *leadership* usually brings to mind guiding those who serve under us (a task he calls "leading down"), but in this address, he broadened that perspective to include leading in three other directions as well—in, up, and across.

"Leading in" means leading oneself. Self-leadership involves living with integrity, possessing self-discipline, taking necessary time to consider vision and goals, and creating positive habits that nip burnout in the bud. George Van Valkenburg's succinct description says it all—"Leadership is doing what is right when no one is watching." We'll discuss this characteristic further when we speak of integrity.

"Leading up" encompasses our pastor, elders, and any others to whom we report. It is important not only to clarify their expectations of us but also to explain how our work with children aligns with church goals and how the whole church will benefit from children's ministry. Our role is to contribute to a working relationship with our supervisors, to help them reach their goals, to recognize when to press and when to back off, and to be a person they can trust.

"Leading across" involves partnering with other staff, coequals, or parents to communicate, share your vision, and team up on projects. This is lateral leadership—helping the people around you, working together, and being a friend devoid of competition. Ralph Roberts says, "You don't need all the glory. If you let others take the credit, it makes them feel like they're part of something special."

Finally, "leading down" may involve your staff or team, volunteers, and the children. Your role in top-down leadership is not one of control. Rather, your call is to empower, inspire, energize, encourage, relate, elevate strengths, transfer the vision, and model the behavior you want to see in others.

INTEGRITY

Some of my dearest friends are of the Catholic faith. They grieve over the negative impact the moral downfalls and cover-ups have had on parishioners, priests, and their church's reputation in recent years. You may know similar stories in our own church body. Major integrity or character lapses have caused lives and ministries in all denominations to come crashing down. What a tragedy when innocent people are hurt, trust is broken, and a witness for Christ is tainted in the eyes of nonbelievers.

But with the subject of integrity, we're not just talking about the big stuff. We are also speaking about the little temptations that come our way each day that challenge our moral principles, our honesty, and our uprightness. Much of this "little stuff" subtly takes place in our own hearts and away from the eyes of outsiders.

One Sunday a few months after I started doing the children's messages in our worship services, the thought went through my mind, "Cynthia, you're finally getting the hang of this." The subtle temptation to self-sufficiency and pride thankfully resulted in completely drawing a blank in the middle of the message. I use the word *thankfully* because that experience reminded me of my constant need to rely on God and direct people to Him, not to myself.

The call to integrity also challenges me to check my motives when we plan outreach events for children. Do I care more about having lots of children attend so it looks like we're accomplishing something, or do I care more about children and their families hearing the Good News of Jesus? At times, this reality check of the heart brings me to my knees in repentance and refocuses my heart on God and His values.

It has been said that one of the greatest indicators of integrity is how we use the authority granted us. Influence can be a gift used to rouse people to more earnestly follow Jesus. Or it can invite power, pride, control, arrogance, or the feeling that nothing can touch us. Do you recall the request the mother of James and John made to Jesus regarding her sons? Jesus responded with a call for servanthood: "You know that the rulers of the Gentiles lord it over them, and their great ones exercise authority over them. It shall not be so among you. But whoever would be great among you must be your servant" (Matthew 20:25–26).

Living an authentic life of integrity does not come by simply muscling up and doing honorable deeds. Few were more upright than the Pharisees in Jesus' day. Focusing on outward behavior alone misses the point of what Jesus wants us to deal with—the inner workings of our hearts. He wants to make us "inside-out people," to clean up our interior personal messes through confession before concerning ourselves with how we look on the outside to others. The road to integrity is the difficult path of repentance.

Jim Wideman said, "Get your own house in order before trying to lead others."[16] When we deal with our own logs before trying to remove specks of sawdust in others, we begin to see God's definition of integrity.

CONFLICT

Desiring to reflect Christ in our lives is particularly challenging and critically important when conflict arises. We may witness the discord between others, or we may be in the center of the disagreement ourselves. Conflict has the potential to grow mistrust and derail ministry, but it also has the potential to build camaraderie and move ministry forward.

A number of years ago, our church conducted four weeklong VBS programs for neighborhood kids and another VBS week for kids bused in from Detroit. If the scenario of five different weeks of VBS sounds like a summer of exhaustion, you're right! Not surprisingly, subtle discord emerged. Some volunteers would only help for the Detroit week because that qualified as true "outreach" in their eyes. Others were frustrated by added confusion during that particular week and would not participate. After choosing to honestly and directly discuss the issues and refocus on our shared goals, a healthy resolution emerged. The city kids were integrated with the neighborhood kids, and all the volunteers were pooled together. The result? VBS was reduced to four weeks (yeah!), volunteers' hearts grew to include a broader spectrum of children, truth was faced, integrity was pursued, and God was honored.

Jack Welch's phrase has been quoted all over social media: "The kindest form of management is the truth." For those of us who want to be "nice" and "loving," we may mistakenly rephrase his statement to read, "The kindest

16 Jim Wideman, *Children's Ministry Leadership* (Loveland: Group Publishing, 2003), 61.

form of management is avoidance." It's natural to want to dodge issues that have the potential to produce tension and ruffle feathers. The word *flight* aptly describes this tendency to be passive.

Others may lean toward the "fight" extreme. Using truth as justification, kindness may be ignored. A person who assumes an aggressive posture and sets his or her goal on gaining a victory usually incites more anger. Resolution becomes even more distant and difficult to achieve.

"Speaking the truth in love," Ephesians 4:15 says, is the means "to grow up in every way into Him who is the head, into Christ." Love is shown through speaking the truth, and speaking the truth is motivated by and graced with love; both are necessary ingredients for resolving relational tension.

Jesus perfectly balanced these two poles. At times He was the catalyst for tense situations, and at other times He stepped into them, but His demeanor was one of dignity and confidence. In holiness and obedience to His Father, the Son of God met these challenges with clarity and assurance. Jesus' composure might be described by the phrase "a less anxious presence," as used in *The Leader's Journey*.[17] We, too, can respond to conflict with poise and self-control when we rest in Him alone as our source of strength.

Conflict resolution brings with it no guarantees. But prayerfully facing issues can be a personal growth opportunity as we desire above all to bring God glory. We cannot control outcomes, but we can regulate our own reactions. "If possible, so far as it depends on you, live peaceably with all" (Romans 12:18).

Children's Ministry Magazine had a timeless article about conflict entitled "Blessed Are the Peacemakers," which shared this apt description: "Conflict is like a gallon of milk. Drink it fresh, or stuff it in the back of the refrigerator and pretend it doesn't exist. Conflict has a limited shelf life. Keep conflict past its expiration date, and bitterness and gossip sour it. A rancid smell will ruin the taste of everything else in your heart's crisper."[18] The milk metaphor continues with five practical steps.

1. Screen it—see if it's worth your energy to be upset.

2. Chug it—embrace it as a divine opportunity to practice peacemaking. Reject the self-indulgent pleasure of being a passive victim.

---

17 Jim Herrington, R. Robert Creech, and Trisha Taylor, *The Leader's Journey* (San Francisco: Jossey-Bass, 2003).

18 Larry Shallenberger, "Blessed Are the Peacemakers," *Children's Ministry Magazine*, July/August 2001, 42–46.

3. Test it—take a clear look at the issue to see if you played any role in creating the conflict. Consider Jesus' picture of a person wielding lumber in his or her eye while trying to remove sawdust from another's eye.

4. Do it—talk with the person in private. If you can't get on the same page, ask a third party to help break the stalemate. If there is a need to tell the church, the goal of restoration remains. At this point, you lose your freedom to negotiate and are subject to the prescriptions of the governing body.

5. Finish it—say the last 10 percent. Deal thoroughly and completely with the conflict to prevent any ill will from lingering and potentially eliciting more bitterness. History teaches that today's wars are born from yesterday's faulty peace.

BALANCE

When my Pilates instructor calls for exercises promoting balance, I am one of the wobbly ones, desperately trying to focus on something fixed in the room to retain stability. Maintaining balance emotionally, mentally, relationally, and spiritually creates similar challenges. It's so easy to lose our equilibrium and find ourselves totally absorbed in some areas of life while minimizing others.

It's been said that because of our fallen nature, we all have one addiction or another. Truth be told, one of mine is workaholism. I don't know who originally penned the phrase "if the devil can't make you bad, he'll make you busy," but it plays itself out in my life in more ways than I wish to admit. As a result, Eugene Peterson's thoughts on the subject are tough to hear: "I am busy because I am vain. I want to appear important. Significant. What better way than to be busy? The incredible hours, the crowded schedule, and the heavy demands on my time are proof to myself—and to all who will notice—that I am important."[19] I, I, I—did you note the focus?

Those of us who serve at church know that work is never done. There is always another call to make, another lesson to plan, meeting to set, and article

---

19 Eugene Peterson, *The Contemplative Pastor* (Grand Rapids: Eerdmans, 1989), 18.

to write. "Doing" becomes more important than "being." The relationships we have with ourselves, others, and even God Himself are negatively affected. An obsession with completing tasks prevents us from becoming the person God created us to be. Not only do we shortchange ourselves, but when life gets out of balance, our families are squeezed as well. We stay late at church or use time designated for the family to finish the day's incomplete tasks. And most serious of all, other priorities have replaced God as number one in our lives.

In *Strengthening the Soul of Your Leadership*, Ruth Haley Barton writes, "God is the one who is infinite; I, on the other hand, must learn to live within the physical limits of time and space and the human limits of my own strength and energy. There are limits to my relational, emotional, mental, and spiritual capacities. I am not God. God is the only one who can be all things to all people. God is the only one who can be two places at once. God is the one who never sleeps. I am not."[20]

With all the people clamoring after Jesus, He surely would have felt the same temptation to overwork. However, the time He spent alone in prayer equipped Him to set priorities and step away for needed rest in order to resume work with vigor and clarity. Keeping His eyes on His purpose provided the stability to maintain His balance. This focus on His Father and the mission before Him enabled Him, when the time was right, to say, "It is finished."

Ruth Haley Barton also writes, "Silence and solitude rescue us from relentless human striving, enable us to give up control and allow God to be God. . . . Rather than leading from a place of frenetic, ego-driven activity, I am leading from a place of rest where I know what I am called to do and I am confident God will produce it. Rather than manufacturing ministry, I am leading from my own experience with God. Rather than being subject to inner compulsions of the self and outer demands of people's expectations, I am learning to respond to God's call upon my life."[21]

Each evening's rest represents God's greater invitation to rest in Him during the waking hours as well. We need to take time to disengage and seek renewal—even the Son of God did that!

---

20 Ruth Haley Barton, *Strengthening the Soul of Your Leadership* (Downer's Grove: InterVarsity Press, 2008), 122–23.

21 Ruth Haley Barton, "Is My Leadership Spiritual?" *Leadership Journal* 27, no. 3 (Summer 2006): 75.

PROBLEM-SOLVING AND DECISION-MAKING

During a recent meeting with a newly created team of leaders, we discussed several options of how to arrive at a particular decision that would affect the entire church. A man who joined the group for the first time spoke his mind, "If this is really a leadership team, then this group needs to make a decision and lead!" He was right. We were dancing around, hoping not to cause offense, wanting to get as many people on board as possible. There's nothing wrong with those desires, but when trying not to cause ripples becomes more important than moving where God is leading, people-pleasing has usurped the first place that only God can claim.

Problem-solving and decision-making provide wonderful faith-growing opportunities, especially for those of us who find them challenging. They are tightly related because solving problems requires making decisions, and decisions are needed because problems emerge. Or perhaps making decisions is the problem!

God's Word speaks with clarity into dilemmas that can stretch our trust in Him. In 2 Timothy 1:7 Paul reminds us that "God gave us a spirit not of fear but of power and love and self-control." We don't have to be paralyzed with doubt when making decisions; He promises to provide all we need. And if any fear is related to displeasing people, God through Paul challenges us with the poignant question in Galatians 1:10, "Am I now seeking the approval of man, or of God?" As beloved children of God, He is the one we ultimately want to glorify.

So whether you need to decide how to handle a disgruntled volunteer or where to locate the new class you're adding, prayerfully ask God for wisdom and discernment.

The following suggestions have been helpful for me and may be for you as well.

1. List the pros and cons of each option. Write down every reason that comes to mind, even those that may not seem important or valid.

2. Prayerfully evaluate the strength and legitimacy of the reasons you have given. Which most support God's kingdom values?

3. Ask God to help you freely choose the option that most clearly brings honor to Him.

4. Take the necessary time for consideration; don't rush the process. Trust God's timing.

I recall a frustrating time at work when neither option A nor option B seemed to be the direction to go. A mentor at the time exclaimed, "What a wonderful place you're in!" What was he talking about? I was feeling backed against the wall! "Option C," he said, "is keeping your eyes on Jesus rather than the immediate circumstances." And Jesus worked through that time in the most creative way imaginable!

CHANGE

"The task of a leader is to get his people from where they are to where they have not been," says Henry Kissinger. And because change will be required along the way, the task can become quite challenging.

Undergoing change is a big deal for most people, especially when the change is *someone else's* idea! Oh, it can be fun and energizing in some settings and for some individuals, but for others, change is threatening and triggers suspicion, resistance, and fear. When leaders underestimate the difficulty of dislodging people from their comfort zones, they can charge ahead too quickly or even impose ideas on people who are resistant. Leaders must learn to identify with those being affected if they want their proposal to have a successful outcome.

Rogers' Innovation Bell Curve gives a visual picture of how various people react to change.

» Innovators represent 2.5 percent of the population. These folks are eager to try new ideas; they are the risk-takers.

» Early Adopters represent 13.5 percent and are influential people whose opinions are respected by their peers.

» Early Majority represent 34 percent. With some deliberation, this people group will adopt new ideas before the average individual.

» Late Majority represent 34 percent. This group is skeptical and cautious about innovation; they adopt new ideas after the average person but can be persuaded with strong pressure.

» Laggards represent 16 percent. The opinions of these folks usually do not sway others. They are fixated on the past and suspicious of innovators. If innovations are eventually adopted, they may already be obsolete.

These, of course, are not hard-and-fast rules. A person's placement on the bell curve greatly depends on his or her belief in the cause. A person in the laggard category might surprise everyone by introducing a new idea. And on the other hand, some innovators could sadly even resist change required by God Himself!

Do you recall previous paragraphs highlighting the critical task of building relationships with people? Personal rapport is no guarantee of success, but it does increase the likelihood of individuals opening their hearts to hear your rationale behind a proposed change. An attitude of humility enables you to ask for ideas, affirm varying opinions, and thank people for their input. As trust is built slowly over time, people will be more willing to listen as you describe problems that need attention as well as possible solutions.

Some people, however, do have negative personalities and seem to thrive on opposition. Do not allow this reality to thwart your desire to follow through with what you believe God has called you to do. People's anticipated reactions cannot determine whether we pursue a change we believe God has initiated.

Use every means at your disposal to help people grasp the vision. Vary your methods of communication. Use words, photos, videos, models, trips, or anything that comes to mind to help people picture the new reality you hope to achieve.

One spring a number of years ago, our Sunday School leadership team attended an out-of-state conference together. We had just joyfully and unanimously concluded that we needed to completely transform our Sunday-morning format, and we hoped to accomplish this feat by September. Yikes! How could we honor the past and yet show our teaching staff the changes that were needed? "Establish a compelling 'why,'" advised a conference speaker. Answering this critical question became our focus. The reasons we discovered and communicated were as follows:

» One hundred fewer children regularly attended than in previous years.

» The mental picture of seeing children eagerly running to enter the church was dampened by the reality of seeing parents coaxing their kids to attend class and friends rarely joining them.

» Our parent survey revealed that some kids didn't come because they didn't know other kids.

» With our self-contained classrooms, some children got in-depth Bible study, others great crafts, others music; it all depended on the teacher's giftedness and interests. We wondered, "What if all the kids could get the best each teacher has to offer?"

» During the welcome calls I made to new families, I increasingly met parents who were "church shopping" and often made their choice based on whether their kids liked being in Sunday School.

A miraculous phenomenon occurred. As we expressed appreciation to our teachers and shared these observations, every single teacher and assistant continued serving through the transition and into the new format the next fall.

Not all stories end on such a happy note. But this experience taught me that initiating change requires proceeding with God-given certainty, wisdom, hard work, and trust.

William Bridges is another author who broadened my understanding of change. His book *Managing Transitions* reveals his preference for the word *transition*.[22] Dr. Bridges suggests that the traditional way of looking at change shows little understanding of people's emotional responses. We usually begin by announcing a date that the proposed change will take place. This beginning step is followed by a time period that allows people to actually process the alteration. Third, we look forward to the end of this transition to allow the new reality to finally emerge. The author suggests that as we look at transition through the eyes of those affected, the stages need to be reversed.

Dr. Bridges intriguingly calls stage one "The End." This is the time of loss and letting go of what was familiar and safe. It can even be looked upon as the

---

22 William Bridges, *Managing Transitions* (Boston: Nicholas Brealey Publishing, 2009).

death of "what was." Understanding that a grief process is inevitable and can even be a healthy response to an ending helps a leader feel compassion rather than anger toward those who express resistance. Emotions such as anger, anxiety, sadness, or disorientation may not be due to bad morale or insubordination after all; people may simply fear what they don't understand. At this stage, empathetic listening and open communication are critical.

His stage two is called "The Neutral Zone." This is the no-man's-land between the old reality and the new. People may experience confusion, resentment, low motivation, anxiety, skepticism, or a lack of productivity. Once again, allow people to talk about their feelings. Short-term goals that result in quick, observable wins can help boost morale as you highlight objectives being attained along the route to change.

Finally, he calls stage three "The New Beginning." This takes place when the suggested change is starting to be embraced. It is a time of acceptance, openness to understanding, and renewed commitment. This is the time to share success stories, to celebrate, to reward hard work, and to keep pursuing the vision God has placed in the heart of His people.

Leading ourselves and others while we follow Jesus can involve maneuvering around the land mine of change as well as many others (and I'm not talking about the dog-training variety of land mines . . . or am I?). One of my greatest blessings through the years has been my spiritual mentor. She has listened, prayed, challenged, and empathized. We have laughed and cried together—well, I've cried anyway. Her not being connected with my churches has given me the freedom to express the good, the bad, and the ugly in my mind and heart. Her experiences, wisdom, and love for Christ have steered me to focus on Him through the rocky terrain called ministry.

Our church body promotes spiritual, emotional, mental, and physical health for our church leaders. And yet, becoming vulnerable is risky, and finding a safe person within our own congregation could be unlikely. I implore you to prayerfully seek out a trusted individual who can serve as a spiritual mentor, one who can walk beside you as you live out your calling to serve the people God placed in your life.

Offering spiritual leadership is such an important vocation. Henri Nouwen holds up the example of the Good Shepherd as our own model for leadership. Jesus says, "I am the good shepherd. I know My own and My own know Me. . . . I lay down My life for the sheep" (John 10:14–15). Nouwen suggests that the same relationship that exists between Jesus and His sheep—us—needs to exist between us and those we lead. He uses words such as *trust, openness, care, love,* and *intimacy.* These words describe how Jesus attends to us as well as how we respond to Him. There is no room for fear or oppression in this give-and-take relationship. May God give us the grace to shepherd others as Jesus shepherds us.[23] May God give us the grace to live out this invitation to shepherd others with the attitude of Jesus.

---

23 Henri Nouwen, devotion for April 13, *Bread for the Journey: A Daybook of Wisdom and Faith* (New York: HarperCollins Publishers, 1997).

* * * *

What is your best leadership advice for a new person in ministry?

1. Start each day in prayer and let the Lord lead you in ministry.

2. Have a set time to meet, communicate, and pray with your pastor(s) weekly.

3. Find a mentor from a neighboring church with a similar program to have lunch with monthly.

4. Spend the first months observing, analyzing, and asking questions about what has been done in the past and is currently happening. (Watch out for sacred cows.)

5. After three months, pick out one or two areas you would like to add or change and concentrate on them.

6. Develop a core team of lay members to help you.

7. End each day in prayer.

Walter Krone
Retired Principal from Guardian Lutheran School
Dearborn, MI

* * * *

A few of us went to the KIDMIN conference a couple of years in a row. That was beneficial to me as someone new in children's ministry. I met others who also ran the church nursery, and we were able to discuss, compare, and contrast our experiences. We were also in an all-day session together called "The Church Nursery." They covered topics such as recruiting volunteers, keeping volunteers, and teaching age-appropriate lessons (YES! Lessons in the nursery!). I couldn't believe they would suggest teaching a lesson to children under 2. They showed us a video of real children, in a real nursery, and it was working! So I came home, pitched this idea to my volunteers (who were skeptical), and then I modeled it for them. Four years later, they still teach a lesson every Sunday. This experience transformed our nursery.

Keri Elliott
FaithKids Preschool Director
Faith Lutheran Church
Troy, MI

* * * *

Realize that you are going to make mistakes and accept that from the beginning. God doesn't use perfect people, He uses willing people. Learn from your mistakes, ask forgiveness (from those you wronged and from God), and move on. Mistakes are bruises, not tattoos.

Carol Zachrich
Woodside Bible Church
Romeo, MI

* * * *

360-Degree Leadership Reflection

	Names of People in This Category	How God Is Calling Me to Improve My Leadership in This Area
Leading In	Me	
Leading Up		
Leading Across		
Leading Down		

Problem-Solving and Decision-Making

STEPS TO SOLVING PROBLEMS

1. Identify the problem

    a. Listen well

    b. Analyze the contributing factors

    c. Bring any fears to God (fear of not knowing what to do, fear of making a wrong decision, fear of conflict, fear of disappointing people)

2. Find solutions

    a. Pray for God's Spirit to open your mind to possibilities

    b. Do not settle for one side or the other—keep pressing for at least a third solution

    c. Consider side effects and long-term effects

3. Choose a solution

    a. Try for a win-win if at all possible

    b. Does the solution bring God glory?

4. Implement the solution

5. Assess the solution

QUESTIONS THAT MAY HELP IN THE DECISION-MAKING PROCESS

1. Does the Bible say anything about this?

2. What would wise advisers counsel me to do?

3. What have I learned from past decisions and experiences that could inform this decision?

4. How is the Spirit prompting me?

5. If a friend asked me for advice about a similar decision, what would I say?

6. What is blocking my freedom to decide?

7. How might I feel about each possible decision five or ten years from now?

What Does the Future Hold?

*"Go therefore and make disciples of all nations, baptizing
them in the name of the Father and of the Son and of the Holy
Spirit, teaching them to observe all that I have commanded
you. And behold, I am with you always, to the end of the age."*
Matthew 28:19–20

Perhaps it was providential that we ended the previous chapter on the topic of change. That is certainly what the future holds, and only God knows what form that will take.

Change abounds in all aspects of life, for children as well as for adults. While growing up, my family always ate meals together, and going to McDonald's was a once-in-awhile Sunday treat after church. Now for many families, going through the drive-through is a more common routine than sitting together around the kitchen table. Television has morphed into live streaming. Reading a book means using an electronic device, even for my ninety-three-year-old father who now reads books on his Kindle! Waiting a few days for a letter to arrive has transformed into waiting a few seconds for a text. Social issues once deemed unacceptable have now become part of our mainstream way of life. When faced with a question as a child, I used to look up the answer in our home set of encyclopedias. Now, my grandchildren simply hop on my lap and ask me to Google information or images for them.

The world in which I grew up was very homogeneous. Now, our neighbors and the people with whom our grandsons attend school are from all over the globe. Many signs in our area that advertise small businesses are written in Arabic. The majority of our local high school scholars are of Asian descent. I recently attended a luncheon with women from my Aqua Fit class who emigrated from India, Iraq, and the Philippines. The places of worship in our city now include a mosque and a Hindu temple.

Yesterday, my husband pointed out that the *Wall Street Journal* included an article on the nearby city of Hamtramck, uniquely situated within Detroit city limits. In the 1970s, 90 percent of the population was Polish; today it is a mere 11 percent. Estimates bring the city's population to over 50 percent Muslim. The Muslim call to prayer has been broadcast for the past ten years. According to this news report, Hamtramck has now elected the first city council in the United States that has a majority of Muslims.[24]

The church culture is changing as well. During my growing up years, all of my parochial school classmates were Lutheran; now at the same elementary school, 68 percent of the students identify themselves as Lutheran. Compared to many of our Lutheran schools across the country, that number is quite high.

The definition of regular church attendance has shifted from attending every week to regularly coming once or twice a month at best. In addition, many people no longer identify with only one church. While holding membership at one church body, they may worship at another congregation to enjoy a change of pace, join friends for an interesting Bible study at another location, and bring their children to a great family event at another. Denominational affiliation is of less importance to families.

LCMS President Matthew Harrison wrote, "The maddening fact is that the Missouri Synod has been in a slow numeric decline since about 1970. The last time a district of the Synod had any increase in its number of baptized was in the late nineties."[25] In addition, the number of young people remaining active in church life after confirmation is seriously decreasing. Even churches in our Detroit suburbs are closing their doors and putting up their properties for sale. As the world's population grows, our US churches shrink.

---

24 Kris Maher, "Muslim-Majority City Council Elected in Michigan," *Wall Street Journal*, November 9, 2015.
25 Matthew Harrison, "Unworthy Servants," From the President, *The Lutheran Witness*, November 2014.

Like it or not, change is seen within our church body itself. Lutheran churches once shared the same page 5 and 15 liturgies; innovation in contemporary settings now offers more variation. Some congregations meet in schools or movie theaters. Some even eliminate the name Lutheran in the hope of preventing unfavorable assumptions by unchurched people.

Yes, the perception of churches and Christian people is changing within our culture. Respect has given way to apathy at best and further to the growing opinion that Christians are judgmental people who need to be avoided.

A changing secular and church culture means that circumstances and issues children currently deal with, as well as those they will face in the future, are far different from what we experienced ourselves. For that reason, no man-made book can fully prepare anyone for what lies ahead.

But how we respond to societal shifts is a decision each of us must make one step at a time. We can get depressed at the changes pressing all around us. We can put our heads in the sand and refuse to adapt. We can become overwhelmed and eventually complacent. Or we can look at the growing mission field in our own homes, churches, and neighborhoods.

Leaders in my own state of Michigan are reaching out to children and families in creative ways that would never have been considered in bygone years. Last summer, new technology enabled our church to host an outdoor family movie night for members and neighbors. Each family was sent home with a gift bag that included a movie discussion that drew the conversation to Jesus. Along with a group of church leaders, I recently watched children perform at a church-owned coffee house in downtown Midland, Michigan. This welcoming (and tasty!) atmosphere sets the stage each day for spiritual conversations with people in the community. Just this morning at my former church, I observed a newly created experience entitled "Discovery Devotions Milestone," designed for parents and children. With the help of a puppet, families were taught how to share, read, talk, pray, and bless one another, the main points of Dr. Rich Melheim's FAITH5.

Hope stirs in my heart. Leaders are looking squarely at the mission field in their own backyards and are actively taking steps to influence families and neighborhoods with the good news Jesus brings. Those aware of the changing landscape are seeking ways to build relationships and serve people within their own communities as well as abroad. The definition of "ministry success" is shifting from number crunching to faithfully living out God's summons.

Each of us can begin with ourselves. We can connect with family, friends, and acquaintances who do not have a relationship with Christ or who are not part of a faith community. Our motivation is not manipulation, but love! We don't turn people into our evangelism projects; we simply love them, do what we can to develop a closer friendship, and serve them because that is how Jesus related to people. He offered hope to those who received it as well as to those who made other choices. As we seek new approaches to connect with children and their families, we do so in ways they can appreciate and embrace. Methods and programs will and must change over time, but the core of the Gospel remains the same. The unchanging news of our unchanging God and His unchanging love for us because of His Son's sacrifice must be communicated in modes that the present culture can understand.

The jokes about children who answer "Jesus" to any question asked in church really do have it right after all. Jesus *is* "the way, and the truth, and the life" (John 14:6). In those holy moments when we desire to follow Him with heart, soul, mind, and strength, God affirms His faithfulness to us and His promises to guide. Energizing your children's ministry (or any other minstry) is ultimately not about an excellent program, the right curriculum, sharp advertising, or well-trained volunteers. These are important factors, of course; but in the end, it's the Holy Spirit who is in the business of revitalization. He guides us to listen to what He would have us do, who He would have us be, how He would have us enter the lives of others. May our ears and hearts be open to heed His call.

* * * *

What trends do you see taking place for the future of the culture or the church?

1. Children's ministry will continue to be a hard area to work in.

2. Churches with Day Schools put so much emphasis on Monday–Friday that other ministries like Sunday School will continue to slowly die.

3. The number of sports and culture activities for young children will continue to make it hard for families to find time for children's ministries.

4. Children's ministries must break away from the way things have been done in the past. To survive, new and creative ideas must be deployed. (Short time periods, active involvement of kids, use of media and technology, etc. must be considered.)

5. Programs must be designed for total family involvement and not have children's programs set in isolation by themselves.

Walter Krone
Retired Principal from Guardian Lutheran School
Dearborn, MI

* * * *

I would like to speak toward youth ministry. I firmly believe in order to have a future of the church we need to mentor and raise up our children in the church. I think most churches have children's ministry in place. However, I see that churches are losing the middle-school- and high-school-age children. As this group of kids mature, they are finding out about themselves and developing their own unique thoughts and beliefs regarding religion separate from their parents. I don't believe we do enough to foster this age group. This worries me because the youth are the future of the church. My church has worked on building relationships with high schoolers and adult leaders. However, I firmly believe we need to be intentional and also equip the volunteers to build relationships. However, with this emphasis on building relationships, often teaching of the Gospel is not the primary focus. This is the critical time of questioning when we need to equip children with the truths of the Bible. I do believe for the older kids in many churches we teach to the trends and fail to address Scripture adequately. I think Scripture is mentioned, touched on briefly, but it is treated as an appetizer instead of a main course. We fail to get into the "meat" of the Bible. Equip these kids with the tools so they can start to learn and investigate the Bible and build their own relationship with Jesus that will last a lifetime.

Cheryl Wajeeh
Faith Lutheran Church
Troy, MI

* * * *

I am always looking at children during church and seeing who does not come to Sunday School. I will then approach that family and invite them to Sunday School. (We actually call it Sheepfold because the children are God's lambs and the sheepfold is a safe, special place to be.) Anyway, there was a special-needs girl who never came to Sunday School. She was going into kindergarten at the time. I had repeatedly tried to get her parents to bring her to class, but they were sure she would not sit long enough. We have a special-needs co-coordinator who was willing to find a mentor for this young girl, but still no response from the parents.

One week they were going out of town and the daughter was staying with the grandparents who also attend our church. I asked the grandparents if they would be willing to give it a try for "Mary" to attend Sunday School. They checked with the parents and they said yes. We got a mentor for her and she did fantastic. I was ecstatic to say the least and figured the parents would be too. They were skeptical that it would happen again. The next week, the dad came and tried to sit with "Mary" and it was disastrous. I was devastated. I called them and asked what we could do to make this work. They were willing to try again, but with the mentor she did great again. She had a mentor for part of first grade, but then it was decided that she did not need one anymore. "Mary" is now in fourth grade and is the first child to come bounding downstairs every week with a big smile on her face! It just makes me so happy and reminds me to never give up.

Janette Haak
Sheepfold Coordinator
St. Luke
Ann Arbor, MI

* * * *

Bibliography

(n.d.). Retrieved from Group Publishing : http://www.group.com

(n.d.). Retrieved from Kids Kount: http://kidskountpublishing.com

(n.d.). Retrieved from Legacy Milestones: http://legacymilestones.com

(n.d.). Retrieved from Love and Logic: http://www.loveandlogic.com

(n.d.). Retrieved from Protect My Ministry: http://protectmyministry.com

Anthony, Michael, ed. (2006). *Perspectives on Children's Ministry Formation.* Nashville: Broadman & Holman Publishers.

Barna, G. (2003). *Transforming Children into Spiritual Champions.* Ventura: Regal Books.

Barton, R. H. (2008). *Strengthening the Soul of Your Leadership.* Downers Grove: InterVarsity Press.

Bridges, W. (2009). *Managing Transitions.* Boston: Nicholas Brealey Publishing.

Collins, J. (2001). *Good to Great.* New York: HarperCollins Publishers.

Covey, S. (1990). *7 Habits of Highly Effective People.* New York: Simon & Schuster.

Csinos, D. (2011). *Children's Ministry That Fits.* Eugene: Wipf & Stock.

Freudenburg, B. (n.d.). Retrieved from Family Friendly Partners Network: http://familyfriendlypn.com

Freudenburg, B. (1998). *The Family Friendly Church.* Loveland: Group Publishing.

Harrison, M. (November 2014). "Unworthy Servants." In *The Lutheran Witness.*

Hendrix, O. (1988). *Management for Christian Leaders.* Grand Rapids: Baker Book House.

Herrington, J. (2003). *The Leader's Journey.* San Francisco: Jossey-Bass.

Holman, M. (2008). *Take It Home.* Ventura: Gospel Light.

Hybels, B. (2000). The 360-Degree Leader. *The Leadership Summit.* South Barrington.

Hybels, B. (2002). *Courageous Leadership.* Grand Rapids: Zondervan.

Jones, T. P. (2011). *Family Ministry Field Guide.* Indianapolis: Wesleyan Publishing House.

Jutila, C. (2002). "Determining and Developing Your Leadership Team." In *Children's Ministry That Works!* Loveland: Group Publishing.

Lloyd-Jones, S. (2007). *The Jesus Storybook Bible.* Grand Rapids: Zondervan.

Maher, K. (November 9, 2015). "Muslim-Majority City Council Elected in Michigan." *Wall Street Journal.*

Maxwell, J. (1998). *21 Laws of Irrefutable Leadership.* Nashville: Thomas Nelson.

Melheim, R. (n.d.). Retrieved from Faith Inkubators: http://faithink.com.

Nouwen, H. (1989). *In the Name of Jesus.* New York: The Crossroad Publishing Company.

Peterson, E. (1989). *The Contemplative Pastor.* Grand Rapids: Eerdmans.

Ranier, T. (2001). *Surprising Insights from the Unchurched.* Grand Rapids: Zondervan.

Rath, T. (2007). *StrengthsFinder 2.0.* New York: Gallup Press.

Shallenberger, L. (July/August 2001). "Blessed Are the Peacemakers." *Children's Ministry Magazine.*

Wideman, J. (2003). *Children's Ministry Leadership.* Loveland: Group Publishing.